Taylor's Pocket Guide to

Herbs & Edible Flowers

Taylor's Pocket Guide to

Herbs
and
Edible Flowers

ANN REILLY
Consulting Editor

A Chanticleer Press Edition
Houghton Mifflin Company
Boston

Taylor's Pocket Guide is a
registered trademark of
Houghton Mifflin Company.

For information about
permission to reproduce selections from this book,
write to Permissions,
Houghton Mifflin Company, 2 Park Street,
Boston, Massachusetts 02108

Based on Taylor's Encyclopedia of Gardening, Fourth Edition,
Copyright © 1961 by Norman Taylor,
revised and edited by
Gordon P. DeWolf, Jr.

Prepared and produced by Chanticleer Press, New York
Typeset by Dix Type, Inc., Syracuse, New York
Printed and bound by
Dai Nippon, Tokyo, Japan

Library of Congress Catalog Card Number: 89-85027
ISBN: 0-395-52246-3

DNP   10   9   8   7   6   5   4

CONTENTS

GARDENING WITH
HERBS AND EDIBLE FLOWERS

HERBS AND EDIBLE FLOWERS are valued for their aromatic and flavorful qualities. Traditionally, herbs and flowers were used medicinally, as well as to flavor recipes, make teas, scent potpourris and sachets, add color to table arrangements, make dyes and rinses, and repel insects. But only the gardener knows the exciting possibilities of the herb and edible flower garden: fresh basil leaves with sliced tomatoes, nasturtium leaves and flowers chopped into a salad, or candied lilacs decorating a cake or served over ice cream.

This book will introduce you to those herbs and edible flowers that are easy to grow, as well as some that are a little more challenging. No matter where you live—country, suburbs, or city—you can grow herbs and edible flowers. Although you can easily buy them in the market, it is infinitely more satisfying to enjoy them fresh from the garden, knowing that you grew them yourself.

What Is an Herb?

Strictly defined, an herb is a flowering plant that lacks a permanent woody stem. In this book, however, we use the word "herb" in the wider, popular sense to refer to plants with medicinal, savory, or aromatic properties in their leaves, stems, flowers, seeds, or roots.

The herbs and edible flowers in this book belong to three different groups, distinguished by their life cycles: annuals, biennials, and perennials. Annual plants grow, set seed, and die in one growing season. Biennials grow for two seasons and usually flower, set seed, and die in the second year. Perennials grow and flower each year; most die to the ground each winter and grow back in spring.

Some tender biennials and perennials can be started early in the year and grown as annuals in areas where they are not winter hardy. Some biennials, such as parsley, are best grown as annuals because their foliage becomes tough or bitter in the second year.

In addition to the "true" herbs, this book also includes several trees, shrubs, and vines—woody perennials—that have savory or aromatic leaves or flowers.

First Steps Toward Planting

There are herbs and edible flowers for every climate, environment, and condition. Whether you are planning a window box, an old-fashioned knot garden, or a kitchen garden, there are herbs and edible flowers to fit your situation. The key to successful herb gardening is evaluating your needs and choosing the right plants to fit them.

Where Does Your Garden Grow?

One of the most important considerations in planning a garden is plant hardiness; that is, a plant's climatic fitness, or its ability to survive in your climate. Plant hardiness is based on three factors: temperature, availability of water, and soil conditions. Temperature is by far the most important factor.

The hardiness of annuals is rated in a different way from that of perennials. Annual plants are usually described as "tender," "half-hardy," or "hardy." A tender annual is a plant that will not tolerate frost or, usually, cold weather. Half-hardy annuals grow well in cool weather and may tolerate light frost. Hardy annuals tolerate heavy frost and can usually be planted in the garden in early spring.

Perennials are rated according to their ability to survive in particular geographical zones. The U.S. Department of Agriculture has divided the North American continent into ten zones, based on average minimum winter temperatures; the hardiness map on pages 106–107 will show you which zone you live in. Zone 1 is the coldest, with winter lows of $-50°$ F, and zone 10 is the warmest, with winter minimums of $30°$ to $40°$ F. If you live in zone 5, any of the perennial herbs in this book that are hardy to zones 1 through 5 will survive the winter in your area. An herb that is hardy to zone 6, however, will probably not survive the winter outdoors in zone 5.

The temperature of every garden, however, is further affected by topographical and architectural features. A garden enclosed by a wall, for example, may be able to support plants that are not otherwise hardy in that zone. A garden on a windswept slope may be cooler than average, and many plants hardy to the zone may not survive there. These variations in temperature, exposure, and the like are known as microclimates.

If you are just starting an herb garden, choose plants that are known to be hardy in your area. With experience, you will begin to discover the microclimates on your property and can then experiment with a broader variety of plants.

Sunlight Requirements

The amount of sunlight that herbs and edible flowers need for growth varies from plant to plant. Many need full sun; there are a number, however, that grow well in partial shade or light shade, receiving only four to six hours of sunlight or dappled shade all day. Refer to the individual plant descriptions for light requirements before deciding which herbs to grow. In areas where summers are very hot, some sun-loving herbs will benefit from partial shade; others that grow vigorously in sun are less aggressive in partial shade.

Soil

The soil requirements of herbs and edible flowers vary as well. Some herbs must have dry soil to produce their most fragrant or flavorful foliage, while others prefer soil with average or moist conditions. Some actually grow best in poor soil—soil that is low in organic matter. And still others need rich soil, which means that a quarter to a third of the soil volume is organic matter. You can increase the organic content of your soil by adding peat moss, leaf mold, compost, or dehydrated manure.

One essential requirement for herbs is well-drained soil. If your soil retains puddles for more than several hours after a rain or watering, you may have a drainage problem. You can improve your soil's drainage by adding organic matter, gypsum, perlite, or vermiculite, or you can grow your herbs in raised beds.

Fertilizer

A complete fertilizer contains nitrogen, phosphorus, and potassium (potash). In commercial fertilizer, the percentage of each of these elements in the mixture is indicated by three numbers on the package. A fertilizer marked 5−10−10, for example, contains 5 percent nitrogen, 10 percent phosphate, and 10 percent potash; the ratio of elements is 1:2:2.

Nutrient requirements vary from plant to plant; refer to the individual plant descriptions for specific needs. Most herbs, however, will benefit if you mix a fertilizer with a 5−10−5 rating into the soil prior to planting, especially if the bed is new. Herbs grown for their flowers or seeds do best with a fertilizer that is somewhat low in nitrogen (with a 1:2:1 or 1:2:2 ratio, for example), while those grown for their leaves will benefit from more nitrogen (a ratio of 2:1:2 or 2:1:1 is fine), because nitrogen encourages the growth of foliage at the expense of flowers or fruit.

The Importance of pH

The pH of soil is the measure of its acidity or alkalinity; pH affects plants' uptake of certain nutrients. The pH is measured on a scale of 1 to 14; 1 is the most acid, 7 is neutral, and 14 is the most alkaline. If you are not sure of the pH of your soil, you can buy a test kit at garden supply stores or have it tested by your county Cooperative Extension Service or a soil testing lab. In general, soils in the East and Northwest are acid, and soils in the Midwest and Southwest are alkaline.

Most herbs prefer a slightly acid to neutral soil, with a pH of 6 to 7. Exceptions to this general rule are noted in the individual plant descriptions. If you choose a plant that needs acid soil, you can lower the pH of your soil by adding sulfur. To raise the pH (to make acid soil neutral or alkaline), incorporate limestone into the soil. Dolomitic limestone is recommended; it does not burn plant roots, and it contains magnesium and calcium, elements essential for plant growth. Many fertilizers are slightly acid, as are peat moss and humus; they will lower pH somewhat.

Getting Started

After you have studied your light and soil conditions, you need to plan the layout of your herb garden. You can grow herbs in a traditional garden, mix them with flowers and vegetables, or grow them in containers. Many herbs are quite attractive and mix well with annuals and perennials. They can be used as borders, edgings, or ground covers. The size and shape of the herb garden depends on your space, overall garden design, and the time you want to spend maintaining it.

You can lay your herb garden out in geometric blocks or wedges or design a more natural form. Before you buy plants or seeds, sketch your garden out on graph paper and try a few different designs. The sketch can then help you to determine how many plants you will need.

Before you begin preparing your soil for planting in spring, test it to see if it is ready to be worked. If you begin to work the soil too early, you can compact it and ruin its texture. Take a handful of soil and squeeze it. If it stays in a tight, sticky ball, it is still too wet; wait a few days and try again. If the ball crumbles easily, the soil is ready. If your soil is dry or dusty, water it deeply several days before you try to work it, and test it as described above.

To prepare your garden site, first remove existing grass and clear away rocks, sticks, weeds, and other debris. Spade or till the area to a depth of 8 to 12 inches. If you are growing perennials, pay special attention to the early preparation of your soil, for the plants will remain in the same spot for several years to come.

If you must add amendments to your soil, such as organic matter, or if you need to raise or lower the pH of your soil, this is the time to do so. Now is also the time to add fertilizer, mixing it in well with a spade or Rototiller. (If you have adjusted the pH, wait two weeks for the adjustment to take effect before adding the fertilizer.) If your soil drains poorly, add perlite, vermiculite, or coarse sand; to improve drainage in clay soil, mix in some gypsum (calcium sulfate), which you can buy at a garden center.

Planting the Garden

Herbs and edible flowers have various planting requirements. Some can be started from seeds sown directly in the garden;

others need to reach the seedling stage in a controlled environment before being replanted outdoors. You can buy seedlings or start your own indoors from seeds. Some herbs cannot be grown from seeds or are not as flavorful when grown that way, so you will need to buy established plants or grow your own from cuttings or by dividing existing plants.

Starting Seeds Indoors

Plants with fine seeds should be started indoors; so should those with a long growing season, because they may not have time to flower or set seed if they do not receive a head start. Most annual herbs, as well as biennials and perennials being grown as annuals, should be started from seeds six to eight weeks before the date they can be planted in the garden. Biennials and perennials being grown as such may be started indoors anytime through midsummer.

To grow seeds indoors, choose containers 2½ to 4 inches deep with drainage holes. Wash and rinse them in 10 percent bleach solution before you use them. You can also purchase flats or packs; all containers except those made of compressed fiber or peat can be reused from year to year. Herbs that do not transplant easily should be started in individual plastic or peat pots, so their roots will be disturbed as little as possible when you transplant them.

Sow your seeds in a soilless medium; garden soil is too heavy, may not drain well, and carries insects, diseases, and weed seeds. You can purchase sowing mix or make your own of 50 percent peat moss and 50 percent perlite or vermiculite.

Never reuse the medium for sowing seeds because it may not be sterile the second time.

Moisten the sowing medium and fill the flats to within ¼ inch of the top. Sow the seeds according to seed packet directions; do not cover tiny ones, and cover larger ones with only ⅛ to ½ inch of medium, depending on their size. Place the container in a clear plastic bag or cover it with glass until germination has occurred. It is not necessary to water during this time. Most seeds benefit from bottom heat during germination, so place the flats on heating cables (available at garden centers) or in a warm spot, such as on top of the refrigerator. Put the containers in light but not in full sun.

Once the seeds have germinated, remove the plastic bag or glass and move the containers into full sun or place them under fluorescent lights for 12 to 14 hours a day. Water as soon as the medium starts to dry out; watering from the bottom is recommended because it will not dislodge small seedlings. You can start fertilizing the seedlings when they have four leaves, using quarter-strength soluble fertilizer. It is a good idea to transplant the seedlings into individual pots or cells when they are at least 1 inch high and have four leaves; doing so will make the transition to the garden easier. Stop fertilizing for two weeks after transplanting.

Before you plant your seedlings in the garden, they must be "hardened off." One week before they are ready to go outside, move the plants into a protected spot outdoors in the shade and bring them back in at night. Each day, increase the amount of light they receive and the length of time they are outdoors, until the week is up and they can be planted.

Seedlings can also be hardened off in a cold frame, which is a bottomless box set on the ground with a removable, transparent top. You can buy a cold frame or make one from wood and an old storm window.

Starting Seeds Outdoors

The right time to sow seeds outdoors depends on the chosen plants' hardiness and whether they are annuals, biennials, or perennials. The seeds of tender annuals should be sown in the garden after all frost danger has passed. The seeds of half-hardy and hardy annuals can be started in early spring to mid-spring; hardy plants will tolerate frost and half-hardy plants will survive light frost. The seeds of some plants can be sown in fall to germinate the following spring. Biennials and perennials can be sown anytime from spring through midsummer.

Before sowing seeds, water the prepared seed bed well. You can sow your seeds in rows or scatter them; seedlings of those randomly sown, however, can be mistaken for weeds. Plant the seeds following packet directions or the instructions in the plant description. Keep the soil moist until the seeds have germinated. Once the plants are growing, gradually reduce watering to about once a week. When plants are 1 to 2 inches high, thin them to the final spacing given in the plant description or on the seed packet.

Buying Plants

If you are going to buy plants, do so as close as possible to the time when you are going to plant them. Look for plants that have good color, show signs of growth, appear healthy, and have no signs of insects and diseases. If you are buying an herb for its leaves, taste a little bit of it first to make sure it has a good, strong flavor, or rub a leaf between your fingers to bring out the scent. If you can't plant your herbs right away, place the pots or flats in partial shade and check them every day to see if they need to be watered.

Planting Dates

When you plant your herbs depends upon the type of plant you are growing. Tender annuals cannot go into the garden until all danger of frost has passed and the soil is warm. Most half-hardy plants can be put in the garden two to four weeks before the last spring frost, and most hardy plants one to two months before the last frost. Biennials and perennials being grown as annuals are usually planted as early in spring as possible. Biennials and perennials being grown as such can be planted in spring or summer, as long as they are in the ground about six weeks before the first fall frost. If you are not sure about the frost dates in your area, ask your county Cooperative Extension Service or your local garden center.

Planting the Herbs and Edible Flowers

Whether you purchase plants or grow your own, the planting procedure is the same. If possible, plant late in the afternoon or on a cloudy day to ease the transplanting shock. Water the plants and the ground. Remove the plants from their containers carefully; try not to disturb the root ball. Turn the container upside down and, if necessary, rap the bottom with a trowel to help remove the plant. Never pull the plants out by their stems. If your plants are in peat pots, peel away as much of the pot as you can, and when you plant, be sure the lip of the pot is below the soil surface.

Dig a hole slightly larger than the root ball and place the plant in the hole at the same depth at which it was growing. Gently firm the soil around the roots. Water well and water again daily for about a week or until you see new growth. Gradually reduce watering to about once weekly.

Caring for the Herb Garden

Now that your plants are in the ground, there are a few simple guidelines to follow for their maintenance. Generally speaking, the plants in this book require only the most basic maintenance—watering, feeding, weeding, and mulching.

Watering

How often you water your herb garden depends on the herbs you are growing and the weather conditions. Refer to the plant accounts for this information. If you have herbs that like dry soil, allow the soil to dry out before you water again. Herbs that require average moisture conditions should be watered as soon as the soil starts to become dry. Keep the soil evenly moist at all times for those that need moist conditions, but keep in mind that many plants lose their flavor or even die if they are over-watered. Under average conditions, watering once a week is sufficient. When you do water, soak plants deeply to encourage a strong root system. Overhead watering with a hose is acceptable, but be sure to water in the morning so the foliage will dry before nightfall (wet leaves are susceptible to disease). Tall and weak-stemmed plants can be damaged by overhead watering; if possible, water these with soaker hoses.

Fertilizing

For many annual herbs, the fertilizer that was incorporated into the soil at planting time is sufficient; no further feeding will be necessary. Other herbs require additional feeding during summer. Many perennial herbs need only a light feeding in spring when growth starts. Check the plant descriptions for specific needs. Use a complete fertilizer such as 5–10–5 and follow the label directions.

Weeding

It is very important to keep your garden free of weeds, which compete with garden plants for light, water, and nutrients, and often carry diseases and insects. Pull small weeds as soon as they appear. This is easiest to do right after a rain or a watering. Mature plantings can be weeded with a hoe. Pre-emergent herbicides that prevent weed seeds from germinating will not harm established herbs; do not use any other type of herbicide. Mulches also help to control weeds.

Mulching

A mulch is a protective covering that is spread over the soil and around the bases of plants to keep the ground cool and moist, to prevent weeds from sprouting, and to give the garden a finishing touch. There are organic mulches, such as bark chips, leaves, hay, pine boughs, and compost, as well as man-made mulches, such as black or clear plastic and newspapers. Organic mulch should not be used on plants that like poor soil, but plastic mulch may be used.

Some perennial herbs need a mulch during the winter to protect them from cold and keep them from being heaved from the soil. You can use oak leaves, pine needles, evergreen boughs, or mounds of soil. Apply the mulch after the ground freezes and remove it as soon as growth starts in spring.

Propagation

There are several ways to propagate herbs and edible flowers: from seeds, by division, or from cuttings. Generally, the most reliable of these methods is the last. Check the plant descriptions for the best way to propagate individual plants.

Rooting Stem Cuttings

Some herbs and edible flowers do not set seeds and must be grown from cuttings or by division. The seeds of some plants germinate very slowly, so rooting stem cuttings is a faster method of propagation. Other herbs, especially hybrids, do not breed true from seeds—that is, their seeds produce inferior plants that may lack the flavor of the hybrid parent.

Take cuttings from plants in midsummer when the new growth is firm. Choose a stem that has four to six leaves and cut it just above a leaf. Carefully remove the bottom two to three leaves and any flowers or flower buds. Put the cutting in a small pot or flat in moistened, soilless medium, the same type used for sowing seeds indoors. Place the cutting deep enough so the nodes you exposed when you removed the lower leaves are covered by the medium. Gently firm the medium around the stem and place the container inside a clear plastic bag in bright light but not full sun. After several weeks, test to see if the cutting has rooted by gently tugging at a leaf. If it seems to have rooted, remove the bag; if not, replace the bag and try again in a few days.

Division

Division is an easy way to increase the number of plants in your garden. Most perennial herbs need to be divided on a regular basis. This might be annually or every two to three years, depending on how quickly the plants grow. Herbs are best divided in early spring to mid-spring, when growth starts, or in fall, about six weeks before the first frost.

Carefully dig up the plant, keeping the root system as intact as possible. If necessary, wash the soil from the roots so you can see what you are doing. Carefully pull the roots apart with your hands or with a trowel or spade. Replant the divisions before the roots dry out. If you are dividing in spring, cut the tops of the divisions back only if the plant has more than several inches of new growth. When dividing plants in fall, cut the plants back by half to compensate for the lost roots. Water the divisions well after replanting and water them daily for about a week if it does not rain. In spring, water until new growth starts.

Controlling Growth

Many herbs, especially those grown for their foliage, benefit from pinching—the removal of the growing tip to encourage branching. Additionally, some herbs will produce more abundant and flavorful foliage if the flower buds are removed (this process is called disbudding).

Some herbs spread by underground stems or roots and can be quite invasive. To control them, you can place a metal edging in the ground to contain the roots or grow the plants in containers plunged into the ground. Some herbs become weedy or invasive because they drop their seeds and easily sprout new plants. You can prevent the growth of these unwelcome "volunteers" by removing the flowers before they set seeds.

Growing Herbs in Containers

Almost any low-growing herb can be grown in a container. Some good choices are basil, oregano, tarragon, lavender, the mints, and chives; Creeping Rosemary and Lemon Thyme are especially good plants for hanging baskets. Choose a container that is in proportion to the size of the mature plant and that has drainage holes. For the growing medium, use a soilless mix of peat moss with perlite, vermiculite, or coarse sand. Garden soil is heavy and may not drain well in containers. For those herbs that like poor soil and will respond negatively to the peat moss, mix garden soil with perlite, vermiculite, or sharp sand.

Plants in containers need more frequent watering than the same plants grown in the ground. Check them often, especially when it is hot or windy. Water herbs that like dry soil when the top inch of the medium is dry. Water those that like average moisture when the surface of the medium starts to dry out. Keep the medium evenly moist at all times for moisture-loving plants.

Fertilizer leaches from containers quickly, so potted plants may need slightly more fertilizer than garden plants. Judge by the way the plant is growing, and be careful not to over-fertilize. If the plants start to grow unevenly, rotate them so they receive light on all sides.

A Note on Plant Names

The common, or English, names of plants are often colorful and evocative: Shepherd's Purse, Golden Marguerite, Herb of Grace. But common names may vary widely from region to region—Angelica and Wild Parsnip are names for the same plant. Sometimes, two very different plants may have the same or similar common names, as with French Tarragon and Winter Tarragon. And some have no common name at all. But every plant, fortunately, is assigned a scientific, or Latin, name that is distinct and unique to that plant. Scientific names are not necessarily more correct, but they are standard around the world and governed by an international set of rules. Therefore, even though scientific names may at first seem difficult or intimidating, they are in the long run a simple and sure way of distinguishing one plant from another.

A scientific name has two parts. The first is called the generic name; it tell us to which genus (plural, genera) a plant belongs. The second part of the name tells us the species. (A species is a kind of plant or animal that is capable of reproducing with members of its kind but is genetically isolated from others. *Homo sapiens* is a species.) Most genera have many species; *Thymus*, for example, has about 100. *Thymus vulgaris*, culinary thyme, is a species included in this book.

Some scientific names have a third part, which may be in italics or written within single quotation marks in roman type. This third part designates a variety or cultivar; some species may have dozens of varieties or cultivars that differ from the species in plant size, plant form, or flower or leaf size or color. Technically, a variety is a plant that is naturally produced, while a cultivar (short for "cultivated variety") has been created by a plant breeder. For the purposes of the gardener, they may be treated as the same thing. *Tagetes tenuifolia* 'Tangerine Gem' is one example.

A hybrid is a plant that is the result of a cross between two genera, two species, or two varieties or cultivars. Sometimes hybrids are given a new scientific name, but they are usually indicated by an × within the scientific name: *Mentha × piperita*, Peppermint, is a hybrid in this book.

Organization of the Plant Accounts

The plant accounts in this book are arranged alphabetically by scientific name. If you know only the common name of an herb or flower, refer to the index and turn to the page given.

Some accounts in the book deal with a garden plant at the genus level—because the genus includes many similar species that can be treated in more or less the same way in the garden. In these accounts, only the genus name is given at the top of the page; the name of the species, cultivar, or hybrid pictured is given within the text.

One Last Word

Now you are ready to begin exploring the exciting possibilities of cultivating and cooking with herbs and edible flowers. Their fresh flavors and bright colors liven up the plainest of recipes, and dried herbs will keep the taste of summer alive in the kitchen throughout the longest winter.

Herbs & Edible Flowers

Anise Hyssop *(Agastache foeniculum)* Perennial

It's related to Hyssop and tastes like Anise, which is how this plant got its name. A perennial hardy to zone 3, Anise Hyssop grows 3–4 feet tall and has oval, pointed, sharply toothed leaves. The flowers are purplish blue, blooming in spikes during the summer. Native Americans used the leaves as a sweetener and to make teas and the roots as a remedy for coughs and colds. Tea drinkers today still use the leaves, dried or fresh.

GROWING TIPS

Anise Hyssop is easy to grow in full sun or light shade in sandy, well-drained soil. Set plants 18 inches apart in mid-spring through summer and divide in spring or fall when needed. Roots spread quickly, but can be controlled somewhat if the soil is poor rather than rich and if little or no fertilizer is used. Anise Hyssop also self-sows easily, so clip flowers off before they seed. Pick leaves anytime for fresh use; to dry them, pick individual leaves or the entire stem and dry on a screen or hang them upside down.

Hollyhock *(Alcea rosea)*

Perennial

A perennial hardy to zone 3, Hollyhock can also be grown as an annual or a biennial. Plants grow from 2–6 feet high, depending on the variety, and have spikes of single or double, papery flowers of all colors except blue. When grown as a biennial or perennial, Hollyhock blooms in early summer; it blooms later when grown as an annual. Use flowers to make fritters and teas.

GROWING TIPS
Hollyhock likes full sun or very light shade and rich, well-drained, warm soil. To grow Hollyhock as an annual, buy plants or start seeds indoors in mid-spring and set them outdoors, 18–24 inches apart, after frost danger has passed. To grow as a biennial or perennial, set plants outdoors in summer; they will probably not bloom until the second year. Fertilize at planting time and every month during the growing season. Water heavily to keep the soil evenly moist. Pick flowers when they are newly open and use them fresh, or dry them on a screen. Remove the base of the petals, which has a bitter taste.

Chive *(Allium Schoenoprasum)*

Pretty enough for the perennial flower border, Chives have tidy, dense clumps of slender, hollow leaves with a delicate onion flavor. The globe-shaped clusters of purple to pink flowers bloom on 6- to 12-inch stems from mid-spring to early summer. The flowers are also very flavorful and can be used in recipes or as a garnish. Mixed with white vinegar, they color the vinegar a rosy hue and give it an oniony flavor. The leaves can be mixed with sour cream, chopped into soups, or substituted for onions in any recipe.

GROWING TIPS

Chives, hardy to zone 3, grow best in full sun or light shade and prefer a rich, moist, well-drained soil. Add plants to the garden in early spring through midsummer, spaced 6–8 inches apart. Fertilize in early spring when growth starts. Every 3–4 years, plants will need dividing. Cut leaves with scissors at any time for fresh use. Leaves do not dry well but they retain their flavor nicely when frozen.

Ramp *(Allium tricoccum)*

Ramp is also known as Wild Leek because the slender underground stems, which resemble scallions, have a strong leeklike flavor. Use them sparingly to flavor meats and greens. Ramp is a perennial hardy to zone 3. Mature plants are 12 inches high and have long, smooth leaves that are 2 inches across, wider than those of most other members of the onion family. After the leaves fade, the plant sends up flowering stalks bearing rounded clusters of yellow-green blooms, which then produce black seeds.

GROWING TIPS

In early spring, plant rhizomes 12 inches apart in light shade and fertile, moist, well-drained soil. Ramp spreads by underground runners to form clumps but it usually is not too aggressive. To harvest, pull the underground stems from the rhizomes and discard the leaves and the outer skin that sheathes the stem.

Garlic Chive *(Allium tuberosum)*

Also called Chinese Chive, Garlic Chive has long, solid grassy leaves that have a mild garlic flavor. Hardy to zone 4, Garlic Chive grows 18–30 inches high, its stems topped with round clusters of white flowers in late summer. The flowers dry well for use in indoor arrangements. The leaves can be used in any recipe as a substitute for garlic.

GROWING TIPS

Plant the tuberous roots of Garlic Chive in full sun and rich, moist, well-drained soil. Plants can be added to the garden anytime from mid-spring through the summer, spaced 12 inches apart. Divide and thin out clumps when necessary, which may be every year, since Garlic Chive is a fast, aggressive grower. Removing the flower heads before they drop seeds will help to keep weediness in check. Cut back the clumps of foliage occasionally to keep the tender shoots regrowing; older leaves become coarse by summer's end. Snip off the leaves at ground level at any time; use fresh or freeze them.

Lemon Verbena (*Aloysia triphylla*)   Shrub

Lemon Verbena is the only herb with lemon-scented foliage that retains its full scent after drying. It is an open-growing shrub with lance-shaped leaves and very insignificant white to pale lavender flowers in late summer. Lemon Verbena is hardy to zone 9, where it can grow 4–10 feet tall. In other zones, grow it as an annual or dig roots in fall and store them indoors over the winter in moist sand in a cool, dark place; naturally, these plants will grow much smaller. Lemon Verbena's leaves are used fresh for teas and dried for potpourris and sachets.

GROWING TIPS

Plant Lemon Verbena in a spot with full sun and rich, sandy, constantly wet, well-drained soil. Where it is not hardy, plant roots after all danger of frost has passed in spring and fertilize at planting time. Where Lemon Verbena is hardy, feed it in spring when growth starts. Pick leaves anytime throughout the summer and dry them on a screen.

Dill *(Anethum graveolens)*

Hardy annuals that are easy to grow, Dill plants have finely divided, light green foliage that is used fresh or dried to season eggs, vegetables, fish, and sauces. Flat clusters of airy, delicate yellow flowers bloom in midsummer on 2- to 3-foot stems. Use Dill seeds, which form after the plant flowers, for flavoring and pickling.

GROWING TIPS

Full sun and slightly acid, moderately rich, well-drained soil are needed to grow Dill. These plants do not like having their roots disturbed; sow seeds in the garden in early spring or late summer. Plants should be 4–8 inches apart so the stems can support one another. Young plants like frequent watering; older plants will tolerate drier conditions. Dill self-seeds easily and can become invasive. Cut leaves at any time before flowering; removing the flowers will extend the harvest period of the leaves at the expense of a seed crop. To harvest seeds, hang flowering stems upside down in a paper bag after the seeds start to turn brown.

Angelica *(Angelica Archangelica)*

Biennial

The leaves of Angelica, the "herb of angels" (also called Wild Parsnip), are used fresh or dried as a seasoning, particularly in drinks, and the stems are often candied (a long, 1–2 week process) or cooked as a vegetable. This aromatic herb grows 6 feet tall and has large, bold, 3-part leaves. A biennial hardy to zone 4, Angelica has flat to rounded clusters of greenish-white flowers that bloom in the early summer of its second year.

GROWING TIPS

Plant Angelica in full sun or light shade in rich, fertile, well-drained soil. Soil should be moist but not saturated and should be slightly acidic. Set plants out in mid-spring; when growing Angelica from seeds, plant them in fall for spring germination. A summer mulch will help keep the roots cool and will result in better growth. Divide crowded plants in the early spring and replant 3 feet apart. Harvest leaves in the first fall or the next spring. For candied stems, harvest stalks in the second year before the flowers open.

Golden Marguerite *(Anthemis tinctoria)* Perennial

Also known as Yellow Chamomile, Golden Marguerite is closely related to Roman and Sweet False chamomiles. Like those of its relatives, the flowers of Golden Marguerite are dried for use in teas. Blooms are also used for dyes and in potpourris. Plants grow 2–3 feet high and are covered in 2-inch, golden-yellow, daisylike flowers in summer. The varieties 'Moonlight', pictured here, and 'Kelwayi' have finely cut foliage and light yellow flowers.

GROWING TIPS

Golden Marguerite is a perennial hardy to zone 4 that prefers full sun and rich, moist, well-drained soil. It is very tolerant of drought once established and doesn't mind high summer heat. It is easily grown from seeds sown in early spring; plants sown late in the season will bloom the second year. Divide plants each spring as growth starts and replant the divisions 15 inches apart. Fertilize lightly each spring after replanting the divisions. Harvest flowers as soon as they are fully open and dry them upside down.

Chervil *(Anthriscus cerefolium)*

Annual

A common plant in French gardens, Chervil, also known as French Parsley, is usually used with other herbs. It is a dainty plant with finely cut, richly aromatic, light green leaves. These anise-flavored leaves are often chopped like parsley and used in French cooking, soups, stews, sauces, and salads. Flat clusters of white flowers bloom in mid-spring on 18- to 24-inch stems.

Growing Tips

A hardy annual, Chervil tolerates heavy frost but will not grow well when nights are warmer than 55° F. It is therefore best grown in spring and fall, and in winter in mild climates. Unlike most herbs, Chervil prefers partial to full shade and likes a sandy, rich, moist, well-drained soil. It is difficult to transplant, so is best grown from seeds sown in early spring as soon as the soil can be worked. Thin seedlings to stand 6–8 inches apart. Mulch the soil in early spring to keep it cool and extend the growing period. Chervil self-sows easily and often acts as a perennial. Pick leaves at any time and use fresh, dried, or frozen.

Leaf Celery *(Apium graveolens* var. *secalinum)* Biennial

Leaf Celery—also known as French Celery and Chinese Celery—is customarily grown as a long-season annual rather than as a biennial, since older plants tend to become stringy. It is grown for the fancy, aromatic leaves that form on its slender, rounded, 12-inch stalks. Use leaves as a garnish or to give a celery flavor to salads, soups, stews, and vegetable dishes.

GROWING TIPS

Seeds of Leaf Celery should be started indoors in late winter and transplanted outside, 6 inches apart, in mid-spring. Plants moved into the garden too early—when there are still extended periods of cool weather—will bolt to seed. Grow in full sun and very fertile, moist, well-drained soil. To harvest, snap off the outside stems when they are 9–12 inches high, before they develop strings; use the leaves fresh.

French Tarragon
(*Artemisia dracunculus* var. *sativa*)

Perennial

French Tarragon, also known as Estragon, is a 3-foot-tall woody perennial, hardy to zone 5, that has dark green, narrow leaves. It rarely blooms; when it does, flowers are yellow and tiny. An ingredient in béarnaise sauce, French Tarragon is also used with fish, chicken, and vegetables, and to flavor vinegar. It may be dried but is better fresh.

GROWING TIPS

French Tarragon must be grown from divisions or cuttings; if you see seeds for sale, they are not for the culinary herb. Before you buy a plant, taste a leaf to make sure it has a distinct flavor. Plant it in full sun, spaced 3 feet apart, in rich, well-drained soil that has average moisture in summer but is dry in winter. Fertilize with fish emulsion in early spring and again in early summer. French Tarragon must have cold winters to grow well. Pick leaves at any time to use fresh; harvest them in early fall to dry. Handle them carefully as they dry, because bruising causes them to lose their essential oil. Dry leaves on a screen or in a paper bag in a warm, dry place.

Borage *(Borago officinalis)*

Both the leaves and flowers of Borage have a cucumberlike flavor and are often added to salads. The flowers are also floated in drinks and punch bowls and may be candied for use on cakes, ice cream, and other desserts. When mature, this decorative hardy annual has coarse, hairy leaves and blue or purple star-shaped flowers that appear in drooping clusters from early summer until frost. Borage grows 2–3 feet tall. Use Borage leaves with caution; large amounts may be toxic.

GROWING TIPS

Borage prefers a spot in full sun or light shade in dry, average to poor soil. Start seeds directly in the garden in fall or early spring, or buy plants and set them 12 inches apart in early spring to mid-spring. Pinch the plants when they are 6 inches tall to encourage bushiness. Plants may become spindly by midsummer; cut them back by half, and they will produce new leaves and flowers. Pick the flowers as they open and remove the inedible hairy sepals. Harvest only young, tender, hairless leaves and use sparingly.

Black Mustard *(Brassica nigra)*

Black Mustard is a frost-hardy annual grown for its seeds, which are dried and ground to make mustard. Leaves, flowers, and young seedpods can also be used in salads. The plants are coarse, with narrow, lobed leaves. Many branches of small yellow flowers appear in summer, followed by sickle-shaped, 1-inch seedpods. In bloom, plants are 4–6 feet high.

Growing Tips

Plant Black Mustard seeds in early spring or late fall, thinning them to 6–12 inches apart. Grow in full sun and fertile, well-drained soil. Black Mustard will become weedy if seeds are allowed to drop on the ground. Young leaves are best; to use mature leaves, strip away the stringy midrib. To harvest seeds, cut stems off at ground level after seedpods have turned brown, but before they split, and hang them upside down in a paper bag. Seeds are covered with chaff, which can be removed by screening them through a sieve. Handle seeds carefully, as they contain a juice that sometimes irritates the skin.

Calendula *(Calendula officinalis)* Annual

Although it is also known as Pot Marigold, Calendula is a different plant from the marigold grown in the flower garden. Like marigold, however, it is a pretty addition to the flower border. Plants grow 6–24 inches tall and have double, daisylike flowers of yellow, gold, apricot, orange, or cream. The crisp petals are often used as garnishes on soups and hors d'oeuvres. Calendula petals are also used in herbal teas, in potpourris, and in rice as a substitute for saffron.

GROWING TIPS

Calendula is a hardy annual that tolerates cool weather, but doesn't grow well where summers are hot. In the South and in hot areas of the West, grow it in fall and spring. Calendula likes full sun and rich, slightly fertile, well-drained soil that is kept evenly moist. Small plants or seeds can be planted 12–15 inches apart in early spring to mid-spring; in hot climates, plant in late summer to early fall and mulch to keep soil cool and moist. Pick flowers regularly for continuous blooms; use fresh or dried.

Caper *(Capparis spinosa)*

Capers are the unopened flower buds of a spiny, tender perennial that is often grown as an annual or a container plant. The buds are used in sauces, butters, cheese preparations, and garnishes; they are often pickled. Plants grow 2–5 feet tall and may be either upright or spreading. The leaves are round; the flowers that develop if the buds are not picked are 2–3 inches across and pink to white.

GROWING TIPS

Plant caper bushes 3 feet apart in full sun and sandy, well-drained—even dry and rocky—soil. Hardy only to zone 9, the plants may not have a long enough growing season to produce flower buds if grown as annuals; sow seeds indoors in late winter, or overwinter plants in containers in a greenhouse or sunny room. Set plants outside after all danger of frost has passed. Harvest the flower buds by pinching them off before they split and show color.

Shepherd's Purse *(Capsella bursa-pastoris)* Annual

Shepherd's Purse has a rosette of stemless leaves at the base of the plant, arrow-shaped leaves along the 1½- to 2-foot stems, and clusters of white flowers that bloom in early summer. The flowers are followed by flat, triangular seedpods that look like purses. The peppery, mustard-flavored leaves and flowers may be added sparingly to soups, stews, and salads. The leaves and stems turn a lovely straw-yellow when dry and are sometimes used to make wreaths.

GROWING TIPS

Shepherd's Purse needs full sun and average, well-drained soil. Set plants 8–12 inches apart in fall or very early spring. A hardy annual, Shepherd's Purse can become very invasive and is often considered a weed. Pick the flowers when they first open; to harvest leaves, cut entire branches to the ground when the seedpods start to form, and use fresh. For wreaths, cut the entire plant.

Caraway *(Carum carvi)*

Caraway is grown for its crescent-shaped seeds, which are used mainly on breads, cakes, cookies, and other desserts. The 2- to 2½-foot biennial plants, hardy to zone 3, can become rangy in growth. They are covered with finely cut, dark green, almost evergreen leaves that, when young and tender, can be used in salads. The white taproot, which resembles a carrot, is edible also. When Caraway is planted in fall, it produces flat clusters of white flowers in the first summer; when planted in spring, it blooms in the second summer.

GROWING TIPS

Caraway is grown in full sun and generally fertile, neutral, well-drained soil. Roots do not like to be disturbed; it is better to sow seeds directly in early fall or spring, spacing plants 6–8 inches apart. Water when the soil starts to dry out, but decrease watering when flowers open. To harvest seeds, cut off the flowering stems in midsummer after the seeds have turned brown and place upside down in a paper bag. Sift seeds through a fine screen to remove the chaff; pick leaves for fresh use at any time.

Roman Chamomile *(Chamaemelum nobile)* Perennial

Roman Chamomile is often confused with Sweet False Chamomile *(Matricaria recutita),* but the two are entirely different plants. Roman Chamomile, a perennial hardy to zone 5, is a creeping, 6-inch plant with gray-green, finely cut foliage; it is equally at home as a ground cover and in the herb garden. Its strongly fragrant flowers are usually daisylike, with yellow centers and white petals, but they sometimes grow without petals. The flowers are used to make a tea that can also be used to lighten blonde hair.

GROWING TIPS

Roman Chamomile likes full sun to light shade and poor, sandy, well-drained soil. If the soil is too rich, few flowers will form. Plant 3–4 inches apart in early spring; mature plants don't like to be moved. Water well when newly planted; older plants will tolerate either drought or high moisture levels. Large plantings can be mowed in early spring to encourage fuller growth. Cutting flowers early also prevents self-sowing. Pick flowers when fully open and dry on a screen in the sun.

Costmary *(Chrysanthemum balsamita)*

Costmary, or Alecost, was used to flavor ale and beer before brewers knew about hops. It was known in early America as Bible-leaf, because churchgoers used it as a bookmark and, it is said, nibbled on it to stay awake during long sermons. The leaves, which are oblong, fragrant, and slightly curled, have a balsam flavor and can be used fresh or dried in salads, stews, or soups. Costmary rarely blooms; when it does, flowers are daisylike, with white petals and yellow centers. Plants grow 2–3 feet tall and are hardy to zone 4.

GROWING TIPS

Costmary is very easy to grow. It prefers full sun, but it grows well, if less vigorously, in partial shade. Soil should be rich, moist, and well drained for most vigorous growth. Costmary grows quickly, so space plants 3 feet apart. It tends to sprawl and can become weedy, so give it little or no fertilizer to keep the plants tidy. To harvest, cut back by half in late summer. Dry the leaves on a screen or between sheets of wax paper in a heavy book.

Chrysanthemum
(Chrysanthemum × morifolium)   Perennial

Garden chrysanthemums, the mainstay of the fall perennial garden, have edible flowers with a tangy, slightly bitter taste that can be used to make teas or to garnish hors d'oeuvres. Plants grow 1–5 feet tall, depending on the variety, and have dull, lobed, or toothed leaves. Flowers, which come in all colors but true blue, may be single and daisylike, double, or one of many fancy forms. Bloom sizes range from button size to 6 inches across. Perennial mums are hardy to zone 5.

GROWING TIPS

Plant chrysanthemums in spring in full sun and rich, moist soil that is well drained. Taller plants will need to be staked. To keep perennial mums looking their best, root cuttings from new growth each spring and discard the old plants. Then pinch out the growing buds until the beginning of July to encourage bushiness and flowering. Plants will begin to flower when nights get long in the fall. Pick newly opened flowers and use them fresh as a garnish or fresh or dried in teas.

Feverfew *(Chrysanthemum parthenium)* Perennial

Feverfew plants are bushy and grow 2–3 feet high. They have lobed, soft-textured, light green, highly fragrant leaves and tiny, daisylike flowers with yellow centers and white petals. Blooms appear throughout most of the summer and are used in dried arrangements, potpourris, and teas; they also help to repel insects.

GROWING TIPS

Plant Feverfew in spring. It grows equally well in sun or partial shade and is hardy to zone 4, as long as the roots are in soil with excellent drainage, especially in winter. Fertilize very lightly each spring when growth starts and divide at the same time if necessary. Plants readily self-sow and tend to become invasive; keep them in bounds by picking flowers before they set seed. Harvest as soon as the flowers open by cutting the branches to the ground and hanging them upside down to dry in a warm area.

Cumberland Rosemary
(*Conradina verticillata*)

The needlelike leaves of Cumberland Rosemary resemble those of true Rosemary, but these plants grow only 12 inches high and spread to 18 inches across. In late spring, they are covered with showy, tubular, two-lipped flowers of lavender-pink or white. The foliage is used in soups and stews.

GROWING TIPS

Plant Cumberland Rosemary in full sun and rich, sandy, well-drained soil. Hardy to zone 6, it withstands heat and humidity and, once established, tolerates fairly dry soils. If necessary, divide clumps in the fall. To harvest, cut branch tips starting in midsummer; leaves are best when used fresh. Cumberland Rosemary is an endangered species and therefore should not be dug or harvested where it grows in the wild.

Coriander *(Coriandrum sativum)*

Annual

A large, coarse plant, Coriander has flat clusters of white or pale pink flowers on 12- to 30-inch stems in late summer, which are followed by white, lemon-flavored seeds that resemble peppercorns. The seeds are used in Indian curries, Oriental stir-fry dishes, and Scandinavian breads. Coriander's finely divided, soft green leaves, which are used in salads, soups, and ethnic dishes, are usually called Cilantro or Chinese Parsley.

GROWING TIPS

A hardy annual, Coriander likes full sun and average, well-drained soil. It must be planted carefully, as the roots do not like to be disturbed; you may have greater success if you sow seeds directly outdoors in early spring. Thin plants to 8–10 inches apart. Water frequently so the ground is always evenly moist. Leaves may be picked anytime and used fresh or dried. To harvest seeds, cut the flowering stalks when the seeds have formed and hang them upside down in a paper bag.

Squash Blossom *(Cucurbita pepo)*

The blossoms of summer squash, regarded by many people as a delicacy, have a cucumberlike flavor. The large yellow flowers begin to bloom in early summer and will continue to flower as long as the plant is healthy and fruits are picked off. If you harvest all of the flowers, no fruits will develop, so allow some flowers to remain and develop into summer squash. Squash blossoms are often fried or stuffed in Italian cooking and can also be chopped into soups.

GROWING TIPS

Summer squash is frost tender, so plant it from seeds or plants after the last spring frost. Place plants in full sun, 4 feet apart, in rich, fertile soil that is moist and well drained. Use black plastic mulch in cool climates to heat the soil, and straw or other organic mulch elsewhere. Be on the lookout for insects and treat your plants immediately if there are signs of pests. Pick flowers when they are fully open and cook immediately, after removing the stamens or pistils.

Lemongrass *(Cymbopogon citratus)*

Perennial

A plant from the tropics, Lemongrass is a truly grassy plant that can reach up to 6 feet in height, although it is often shorter, depending on the length of the growing season. Because it is tropical, it must be grown as an annual in the U.S.; it likes a long, hot summer. Lemongrass blades are used commercially to distill an oil used in perfumes and flavorings. The gardener can use this plant fresh in stir-fry and fish dishes and teas, or dried in potpourris.

GROWING TIPS

Plant Lemongrass in full sun and sandy, moist, well-drained soil. Set plants 2 feet apart, 2 weeks after all danger of frost has passed. Feed every 2 months with a soluble fertilizer, or every 2 weeks if grown in a container. Cut leaves at any time for fresh use, or spread them on a screen to dry, preferably in a dark place to preserve their green color.

Clove Pink *(Dianthus caryophyllus)* Perennial

Wild Clove Pinks, from which the modern carnation cultivars have been developed, grow 1½–3 feet high and have gray-blue foliage and fragrant, semidouble flowers of rose-purple or white. Depending on the climate, the blooms appear in the cool weather of spring or fall. A perennial hardy to zone 8, Clove Pink can be grown as an annual if started indoors from seeds or from purchased plants. Flowers are very fragrant and are used fresh to flavor syrups, fruit cups, and beverages; they may also be dried for potpourris and sachets.

GROWING TIPS

Set Clove Pinks in the garden 2–3 weeks before the last spring frost, spacing plants 12 inches apart in full sun and rich, moist, well-drained soil. Remove flowers regularly to increase the blooming period; plants will burn out in hot, humid summers, but a mulch may extend their lives. Pick flowers when they are newly opened; remove the bitter white base of the petals before using them. The flowers can be dried in a desiccant such as silica gel.

Sweet Fennel *(Foeniculum vulgare var. dulce)* Perennial

Sweet Fennel may taste like Anise, but it looks more like a large Dill plant, with finely cut, bright yellow-green leaves. Fresh leaves are used in soups, salads, and fish dishes, but they do not dry well. Seeds are used in baked goods and in sausages. Stalks are often burned with charcoal to flavor grilled fish, and some people claim that snacking on fennel stalks reduces their appetites. Perennial to zone 8, Sweet Fennel is usually grown as an annual. Plants grow 4–6 feet tall and have flat clusters of yellow flowers in summer.

GROWING TIPS

Sweet Fennel needs full sun and rich, alkaline, well-drained soil; it tolerates a wide range of moisture levels. Plant outdoors after frost danger is over, spacing plants 8–12 inches apart; handle plants carefully, as they resent transplanting. Prune and feed often to maintain vigor. Pick leaves before the flowers open; to harvest seeds, hold the flower heads over a paper bag and gently tap off the ripe seeds. Grow fennel in an isolated spot, as it interferes with the growth of other plants, especially herbs.

Sweet Woodruff *(Galium odoratum)*

Perennial

Long used as the flavoring for May wine, Sweet Woodruff leaves are also used dried in pillows and sachets to prevent musty odors. The leaves have no scent when fresh, but smell of newly mown hay when dried. Hardy to zone 5, Sweet Woodruff is an attractive, spreading plant that grows 6–12 inches tall, with loose clusters of white star-shaped flowers in late spring. You may see it listed as *Asperula odorata*.

GROWING TIPS

A woodland plant, Sweet Woodruff likes partial to full shade and a rich, moist, well-drained, acid soil. Set plants out in mid-spring, spaced 6–12 inches apart. After the plant has flowered, cut it back to encourage bushiness, but don't give it any fertilizer. Pick leaves before the plant flowers and dry them on a screen in a cool place.

Sunflower *(Helianthus annuus)*

Sunflower seeds are nutritious and are favored by children and adults as well as birds. Sunflowers are coarse tender annuals ranging from 12 inches to 12 feet high, depending on the variety. All have hairy leaves and large, daisylike yellow flowers that form edible seeds.

Growing Tips

Plant sunflower seeds 1–2 weeks before the last spring frost; the seedlings will tolerate light frost. They should be grown in full sun in a warm spot where soil is light and well drained. Fertilize little, if at all, and water sparingly. Seeds of the large varieties should be spaced 4 feet apart, and the plants will require staking or other supports; smaller varieties can be used in the flower garden as decorative plants, spaced 12 inches apart. To prevent birds from pilfering seeds, wrap cheesecloth around the plants or flower heads when seeds start to form. When seeds are hard, cut the stems 6 inches below the flower heads and hang the heads indoors to complete drying. Seeds may be eaten fresh or roasted.

Daylily (*Hemerocallis*)

Perennial

The dried flower buds of daylilies are called Golden Needles in Oriental cooking. The flowers of all daylilies are edible, but not all taste good, so sample a little piece before you dry a large amount. Fresh flowers can also be chopped into salads or soups. The flowers are funnel shaped, from 2–6 inches wide, and bloom on 1½- to 5-foot stems, depending on the variety; blooms may be yellow, gold, orange, or red. The variety 'Admiral Nelson' is shown. Each flower lasts only a day but is quickly replaced by another. The basal leaves are narrow and arching.

GROWING TIPS

Daylilies are hardy to zone 3 and grow best in full sun to partial shade where soil is moist and well drained, although they will tolerate a wide range of growing conditions. Plant in fall or early spring, 18–24 inches apart. Daylilies increase quickly and will need division every 2–3 years. Pick flower buds after they have elongated but before they open and dry on a screen in the sun, or use fresh flowers when they open. Note that *Hemerocallis* lilies are edible, but the similar *Lilium* are not.

Sweet Rocket *(Hesperis matronalis)*

Biennial

Sweet Rocket, or Dame's Rocket, is grown for its fragrant lavender, purple, or white flower sprays, which impart a tangy flavor when used in salads and fruit dishes. Hardy to zone 4, Sweet Rocket may bloom the first spring where seasons are long; elsewhere it will bloom the second. Plants are 3–4 feet tall and have oval, pointed, toothed leaves, which may also be used, along with the seedpods, in soups and stews. Sweet Rocket is related to mustard and has a similar flavor.

GROWING TIPS

Plant Sweet Rocket in light shade and moist, well-drained soil. It dislikes high humidity and grows best where summers are cool. Set seeds or plants into the garden, 12–18 inches apart, in late fall or early spring and fertilize heavily. Sweet Rocket can become weedy if flowers are allowed to set seed. Pick leaves, stem tips, flowers, or seedpods at any time and use fresh.

Rose Mallow (*Hibiscus moscheutos*)

Perennial

A perennial hibiscus hardy to zone 5, Rose Mallow can also be grown as an annual. It grows 1½–6 feet tall, depending on the variety, and has hairy leaves and 4-inch, single, funnel-shaped flowers of red, pink, or white. The flowers, which have a tart lemony flavor, are used fresh in many ethnic dishes, and fresh or dried in hot or iced teas.

Growing Tips

If you are growing Rose Mallow as a perennial, plant it in spring or summer; where it is grown as an annual, seeds should be started indoors in late winter so that the plants will have time to bloom. Hibiscus plants are bushy, so separate seeds or seedlings by a distance equal to the eventual height of mature plants. They like full sun or light shade and rich, moist, well-drained soil of average fertility. They will tolerate high summer heat as long as they are well watered. Provide winter protection where temperatures drop below 20° F. Prune back in spring as needed. Pick flowers when they first open and use them fresh or dry them on a screen.

Hyssop *(Hyssopus officinalis)*   Perennial

At one time, Hyssop was strewn on floors to freshen stale air. Today its leaves and flowers are used by monasteries to flavor liqueurs, and in teas to relieve sore throats and colds. Hyssop grows 18–24 inches tall and can be clipped to a neat, compact shape; it is used as a border or hedge plant in a formal herb or knot garden. A semievergreen hardy to zone 3, Hyssop has dark green, aromatic leaves and spikes of blue-violet, white, or pink flowers in early summer.

GROWING TIPS

Hyssop grows best where frost occurs during winter. It likes full sun to light shade and dry to average, alkaline, well-drained soil. Plants grown in rich soil will have weak fragrance and flavor. Set plants into the garden in spring or summer, 18 inches apart. Divide in mid-spring or early fall if necessary; if dividing is not needed, cut the plants to the ground each spring or fall. Fertilize lightly with fish emulsion when growth starts and after harvest. Pick leaves and flowers when plants start to bloom and dry them.

Bay *(Laurus nobilis)*

Shrub

Used by the Romans in their garlands, Bay—also called Bay Laurel and Sweet Laurel—is a large shrub or tree hardy to zone 8. In colder climates, Bay can be grown as a tub plant and moved indoors in the winter; it will reach a height of several feet. Neither the greenish-white flowers that bloom in early summer nor the greenish-black berries that follow are particularly attractive; the plant is chiefly grown for its aromatic foliage. These leathery evergreen leaves are used whole in soups, stews, and many other long-cooking dishes.

GROWING TIPS

Outdoors, place Bay in full sun or partial shade in rich, well-drained soil. Water heavily in spring, but keep dry the rest of the year. Prune or shear the plant in summer into a hedge, topiary, or other tightly clipped form. Indoors, give it full sun and feed and water it sparingly during the winter. Cut leaves at any time to use fresh, or dry them on a screen or between sheets of waxed paper in a heavy book.

English Lavender *(Lavandula angustifolia)*

Hardy to zone 5, English Lavender is a mounded, fragrant perennial with gray-green, needle-like foliage and narrow 18- to 24-inch spikes of purple-blue flowers that bloom during the summer. Although the flowers are edible, they are bitter and are best left for garnishes, teas, sachets, potpourris, bath salts, and soaps. Equally at home in the perennial or herb garden, lavender also works well as a low hedge or border plant. Popular varieties of English Lavender are 'Munstead' and the deep purple 'Hidcote'.

GROWING TIPS

Lavender grows best in full sun and light, sandy, alkaline soil. Rich, fertile soil produces less fragrant plants. Soil should be kept dry and must be well drained, especially in winter. Add plants to the garden in spring or summer, spacing them 12 inches apart. Fertilize very lightly in early spring when growth starts. Prune back after flowering to keep plants compact and divide them frequently. Pick flowers as they open and hang them upside down to dry in a dark, airy place.

Lovage *(Levisticum officinale)*

Lovage, or "Love Parsley," looks like a large celery plant and has a similar flavor. Hardy to zone 3, Lovage has 2- to 3-foot mounds of leaves that are used fresh or dried in salads, soups, or stews. Six-foot stalks are topped by clusters of greenish-yellow flowers in summer. The hollow stems are used like celery; seeds are used whole or crushed on breads or meats.

GROWING TIPS

Plant Lovage in full sun or partial shade in rich, moist, well-drained soil. This herb must have freezing temperatures in winter and does not like high summer heat. Set plants 12–15 inches apart in early spring as soon as nights remain above 40° F. Fertilize in spring when growth starts and again in summer if the leaves turn yellow. When necessary, divide in early spring or late fall. Pick young leaves for fresh use by removing the outside stalks, or cut the entire stem back before the flowers bloom and dry leaves on a screen. When the seeds turn tan, hang the seed heads upside down in a paper bag to dry.

Honeysuckle *(Lonicera)*

Shrub, Vine

Children (and adults, too) have always delighted in picking honeysuckle flowers and drawing out the drops of sweet juice inside. A shrub or vine hardy to zone 3 and growing 8–10 feet tall, honeysuckle bears flowers of yellow, white, pink, or red during spring and early summer. The blooms have a strong, sweet floral taste and are used in syrups, puddings, and sparingly in ice cream. Berries that attract birds form in the fall. Japanese Honeysuckle *(L. japonica)*, seen here, can be invasive if not pruned.

GROWING TIPS

Honeysuckles are relatively easy to grow, doing well in sun or partial shade and average, even poor, soil. They look their best if the soil is kept evenly moist throughout the summer. Honeysuckles tend to get twiggy in their growth; prune away dead branches and stems each year either before or after the plant blooms. Pick the flowers as soon as they open and use them fresh.

Sweet Bay *(Magnolia virginiana)*

Tree

Leaves of Sweet Bay are often used as a substitute for Bay Laurel but are not as flavorful. They should be used fresh, because they retain little flavor when dried. Leaves are 3–5 inches long, gray-green on the upper surfaces and white on the undersides. Hardy to zone 4, where it grows 1–2 feet tall, Sweet Bay remains evergreen and grows larger, up to 60 feet tall, in zones 8–10. The fragrant, pale yellow to white, cup-shaped, waxy flowers bloom in summer.

GROWING TIPS

Plant Sweet Bay in full sun or partial shade in late winter or early spring, in rich, moist soil that is slightly acid and well drained. Fertilize each spring when new foliage starts to form. Prune the plant after it flowers. Use the leaves fresh anytime.

Mallow *(Malva sylvestris)*

Biennial

A biennial to zone 4 often grown as an annual, mallow grows 3–4 feet tall and has round to heart-shaped, lobed leaves. Clusters of pinkish 1-inch flowers with dark veins bloom in spring or summer, depending on whether the plant is grown as a biennial or an annual. Mallow has been used medicinally since ancient times. Leaves are used fresh in teas; green seed capsules and chopped flowers are used fresh in salads.

GROWING TIPS

Plant mallow seeds or purchased plants outdoors in late spring, setting them 24 inches apart in full sun and moist, fertile, acid soil. *Malva* grows best in cool climates but will tolerate heat if it is well watered. The leaves can be picked for fresh use at any time; to use the flowers fresh, pick them when they open. Allow some flowers to form seed capsules, and harvest them before they split open.

Sweet False Chamomile *(Matricaria recutita)*   Annual

Unlike its perennial relative Roman Chamomile, Sweet False Chamomile (also known as German Chamomile) is an annual, growing 2–2½ feet tall. The leaves, which are apple scented, are gray-green and lacy; flowers are daisylike with white petals and yellow centers, and bloom all summer except where it is very hot. The flowers are used to make herbal tea.

GROWING TIPS

Plant Sweet False Chamomile in early spring, setting plants 8 inches apart in full sun and poor, sandy, well-drained soil. Plant with care, as roots don't like to be disturbed. Once established, these hardy plants tolerate either dry or moist soil. Annual chamomile may self-sow and act as a weedy perennial unless flowers are removed before they set seed. Pick flowers when they are in full bloom and dry them on a screen in the sun. Watch for insects that hide in the flowers; if they appear during drying, rinse flowers in hot water.

Lemon Balm *(Melissa officinalis)* Perennial

Lemon Balm has crisp, lemon-scented, deeply ridged leaves; use them fresh or dried in teas, jellies, fruit salads, and cold drinks. Lemon Balm oil is used in furniture polish; rub fresh leaves on wooden surfaces to impart the same fragrance and gloss. These neat plants grow 2 feet tall and have whorls of white flowers in summer.

GROWING TIPS

Plant Lemon Balm in light shade in poor to moderately fertile soil that is sandy and well drained. This herb prefers moist conditions but will tolerate drought. Hardy to zone 4, Lemon Balm does not grow well in the hot, humid areas of the South. Set out plants anytime during spring or summer, spacing them 18 inches apart. Divide when plants become crowded. After plants have flowered, shear them back to keep them compact. Keep invasive growth in check with an underground barrier. To harvest leaves, cut stems to the ground before the plant blooms and hang them upside down in a hot room; do not bruise the leaves.

Peppermint *(Mentha × piperita)* Perennial

Peppermint, a perennial hardy to zone 3, is the best mint for drying. Plants grow 1–3 feet tall and have smooth, strongly fragrant, 3-inch leaves. Purple flowers bloom in spikes at the branch tips in early fall. Fresh leaves are used as a garnish and in salads or jellies; sprigs placed in cold drinks add a zesty flavor, while dried leaves are often used to make teas.

GROWING TIPS

Peppermint should be started from cuttings, divisions, or purchased plants, because plants do not come true from seeds. When buying plants, taste a little bit of the leaf to make sure you like the taste. Plant 12–24 inches apart in full sun or light shade in spring or fall. Mint prefers deep, rich, open soil that is moist and well drained. Fertilize lightly after plants are harvested. Thin plants every spring; place an underground barrier around them to keep them from becoming invasive. Pinch growing tips off at any time and use the leaves fresh. To dry, cut stems before plants flower and hang them upside down in a cool place.

English Pennyroyal *(Mentha pulegium)*   Perennial

A perennial hardy to zone 3, English Pennyroyal is a spreading plant that grows 6 inches tall and bears spikes of lavender-blue flowers in summer. Its dark green leaves have a pungent, citronella scent and are used in potpourris and as an insect repellent. Pennyroyal can be used in teas and as a flavoring, but only in small amounts as large quantities are believed to be toxic. A close relative, American Pennyroyal *(Hedeoma pulegioides),* is an upright annual growing 12 inches tall.

GROWING TIPS

Growing equally well in full sun or light shade, pennyroyal likes rich, sandy, moist, well-drained soil and grows best where summers are cool. Add plants to the garden from midspring to midsummer, spacing them 1–2 feet apart. Fertilize at planting time and again each summer after harvest. Roots spread quickly but can be contained by an underground barrier. Yearly division will also keep plants within bounds. Dry leaves by hanging stems upside down in a cool spot.

Spearmint *(Mentha spicata)*

Grown as a perennial to zone 3, Spearmint is the most commonly cultivated mint. It grows 1–2 feet tall and has fragrant, toothed, wrinkled leaves, 2½ inches long. Small lavender flowers appear in summer on 4-inch spikes. Use fresh leaves as a garnish, in salads, to make mint jelly, in hot tea, or to flavor cold drinks. The strongly scented cultivar 'Kentucky Colonel' is the favorite for mint juleps.

GROWING TIPS

Spearmint can be grown from cuttings taken in summer, from plants divided in spring, or from seeds. Set plants 12–24 inches apart in full sun or light shade. Mint grows best where soil is deeply prepared, rich, open, moist, and well drained. After plants are harvested, fertilize lightly. Spearmint can become weedy but may be kept in bounds by an underground barrier or yearly thinning. Snip off growing buds at any time and use the leaves fresh.

Bee Balm *(Monarda didyma)*

A tall, stately perennial hardy to zone 4, Bee Balm (also called Bergamot and Oswego Tea) has hairy, mint-flavored leaves that are used in teas, salads, and jellies. Equally attractive in the flower garden and in the herb garden, it has whorls of tubular flowers, appearing in early summer to midsummer, that may be red, pink, purple, salmon, or white. Plants reach 2–4 feet in height and can spread quickly by underground runners to form a large clump.

Growing Tips

Grow Bee Balm in full sun to light shade in sandy, neutral, well-drained soil. It can be quite invasive, but can be kept under control if the soil is dry, poor, and not fertilized. Underground barriers will also help to keep growth in check. Set plants into the garden in midspring to late spring, 12 inches apart. Yearly division and replanting in either spring or fall may be necessary. Bee Balm freely self-seeds, so pick flowers as soon as they start to fade. Pick leaves anytime; they are best used fresh.

Sweet Cicely *(Myrrhis odorata)*

Hardy to zone 3, Sweet Cicely (also known as Sweet Chervil and British Myrrh) prefers cold climates and a woodland setting. The plants look like large Chervil; they have soft, fernlike foliage and 2- to 3-foot stems that bear clusters of small white flowers in mid-spring to late spring. Sweet Cicely tastes like Anise; its leaves, stems, and seedpods are edible. Use it fresh in salads, soups, pies, and teas; eat the seedpods like candy; or dry it for potpourris.

GROWING TIPS

Plant Sweet Cicely in light to partial shade, in soil that is rich, moist, and well drained. To grow it from seed, keep the seeds in the refrigerator for 2–3 months before sowing, or sow them outdoors in fall for germination the following spring. Plant carefully, 12 inches apart, in mid-spring. As roots do not like to be disturbed, plants are difficult to divide; if they become crowded, take cuttings and discard the original plant. Pick leaves or stems at any time for fresh use; collect the seedpods after the plants flower.

Catnip *(Nepeta cataria)*

When the fuzzy gray-green foliage of Catnip is bruised or rubbed it releases an oil that exerts a powerful influence on cats (even though the plant's allure is undetectable to us). Dried Catnip leaves are used in making toys for cats; some people use Catnip to make a pleasant tea that is said to be a comfort for a head cold. Hardy to zone 3, Catnip grows 2–4 feet tall and can spread to cover a wide area. Spikes of flowers are blue or white and bloom in early summer.

GROWING TIPS

Full sun or partial shade is suitable for Catnip, which tolerates a wide range of wet or dry, poor or rich soil, and needs little or no fertilizer. Set plants or seeds into the garden after the last spring frost; since handling plants releases the oil, plant seeds to attract fewer cats. Divide in mid-spring or early fall and space plants 18–24 inches apart. Cut back after the first bloom for a second flowering and cut to the ground every spring. Pick leaves before the flowers bloom and use them fresh or dried.

Black Cumin *(Nigella sativa)* Annual

Black Cumin goes by many other popular names, including Nutmeg Flower, Roman Coriander, Fennel Flower, and Black Caraway. It has 12- to 18-inch mounds of lacy foliage resembling the finely cut foliage of fennel or Coriander. A tender annual, Black Cumin is often grown as a substitute for Cumin *(Cuminum cyminum),* which is slow to develop and needs a very long growing season. The flowers are 1½ inches across and blue or white. The seeds, which form in inflated seedpods, have a spicy, pungent taste and are often used on breads and cakes. Seeds can also be ground and used as a substitute for pepper.

Growing Tips

Plant Black Cumin seeds in the garden 2–3 weeks before the last spring frost. Select a spot with full sun and fertile, well-drained soil. Thin the plants to stand 12 inches apart. Pick the seedpods after they start to turn yellow and dry them in the sun in a paper bag. Put the seeds through a sieve to remove the chaff.

Basil *(Ocimum basilicum)* Annual

It's hard to imagine Italian cooking without basil. The leaves of the variety Fine-leaf Bush Basil are favored for pesto. This versatile herb is used in many non-Italian dishes as well and adds flavor to green salads and fresh tomatoes. As decorative in the garden as it is useful in the kitchen, basil grows 15–24 inches tall and bears spikes of whitish to purplish flowers throughout the summer and fall. The oval, pungent leaves may be green or purple. There are many varieties, including some with lemon, anise, and cinnamon flavors.

GROWING TIPS

Basil should not be planted until well after all danger of frost has passed in spring, because it is one of the least frost-tolerant annuals. Space plants 10–12 inches apart in full sun and dry, light, medium rich soil that is evenly moist and well drained. Fertilize at planting time, and pinch growing tips when plants are 4–6 inches high to induce bushiness. Pick leaves at any time to use fresh; you can increase the harvest if you don't allow flowers to form. To dry leaves, pick them before flowers open.

Holy Basil *(Ocimum canum)*   Annual

This plant, formerly called *O. sanctum*, is so unlike basil in appearance, scent, and flavor that you have to look closely at the flowers to see that the two are related. Holy Basil, also called Hoary Basil or Tulsi, has a heavy, musky, sometimes unpleasant odor that permeates the air and clings to the hands and clothing. Plants grow 2 feet tall and have arching branches covered with hairy gray-green leaves and spikes of dull, bronzy lavender flowers in summer. The leaves can be used fresh, but sparingly, in poultry dishes.

GROWING TIPS

Before buying Holy Basil plants, taste or smell the leaves—some people find them unpalatable. Like basil, Holy Basil is very tender and is not planted until all danger of frost has passed. Space plants 12 inches apart in full sun and dry, light, medium rich soil that is evenly moist and well drained. Pinch growing tips to keep the plants more compact, as they tend to spread widely. Holy Basil can become weedy from dropped seeds, so clip off flowers before seeds set. Pick leaves for fresh use at any time.

Oregano *(Origanum)*

Few plants are more confusing to the gardener than oregano. The dried oregano sold in supermarkets is a blend of different herbs, including oregano, thyme, and others; the garden plants sold as oregano include a variety of species, some of which are often grown as annuals. Most grow 1½–3 feet tall and have fragrant, hairy leaves and purple, pink, or white flowers from mid-summer through fall. Italian Oregano, *O. onites* (pictured here), has a light, warm flavor; Greek Oregano, *O. heracleoticum*, has the most flavor.

GROWING TIPS

Oregano likes full sun and light, well-drained, alkaline soil. Look for plants with a strong, pleasant fragrance. Plant 12 inches apart in late spring after frost danger has passed. Fertilize at planting time and each spring when growth starts. Winter protection is recommended. Plants may be divided in spring; if you find a plant whose flavor you especially like, you can propagate it by stem cuttings. Cut stems back to half their length when flowers open and hang them upside down in a cool place to dry.

Sweet Marjoram *(Origanum majorana)* Perennial

Sweet Marjoram is technically a perennial, but is hardy only in zones 9–10, and is therefore usually grown as a hardy annual. A relative of oregano, it has oval, slightly velvety, fragrant 1-inch leaves that are used in Italian dishes and to flavor meats and vegetables. The tiny pinkish-white flowers bloom in midsummer on plants 8–10 inches in height.

GROWING TIPS

Plant Sweet Marjoram in full sun where soil is light, slightly rich, sandy, and well drained. Water as soon as the soil starts to dry out to keep it slightly moist at all times. Seeds are best started indoors because they are very tiny; set plants into the garden, 6–8 inches apart, in early spring to mid-spring and fertilize lightly at planting time. Pick leaves at any time until the plant blooms for fresh or dried use; dry them on a screen if desired. Removing flower buds will extend the harvest period of the leaves.

Corn Poppy (*Papaver rhoeas*) Annual

The poppy of Flanders Field, Corn Poppy (also known as Shirley Poppy and Flanders Poppy) has dark green, hairy, irregularly lobed leaves and slender, branching stems. The flowers, which usually bloom 1 to a stem, have 4 petals and come in red, purple, pink, and sometimes white. In bloom, plants are 1½–3 feet tall. The fresh petals can be used to color wine or clear syrups, but poppies are usually allowed to form seeds, which are sprinkled on baked goods.

GROWING TIPS

Plant poppy seeds in late fall or early spring, as these hardy plants need a long, cool growing period to develop to a good size before blooming. Plant 8–12 inches apart in full sun in sandy, rich, well-drained soil. Mulch in early spring to keep the ground cool. Pick fresh flowers at any time. To harvest seeds, cut the vase-shaped seedpods as they start to dry and turn color; store them in a paper bag until they are fully dry. Screen the seeds through a sieve to remove the chaff.

Scented Geranium *(Pelargonium)*

Perennial

Although scented geraniums are perennials, they are hardy only to zone 9 and are usually grown as houseplants or annuals. All have loose clusters of white, pink, or purple flowers in summer on 1- to 4-foot plants but are grown mainly for their foliage. Some have leaves that are large and velvety; in other species the leaves are finely cut. The scent, which is released in the hot sun or by rubbing the leaves, varies from lemon to nutmeg, apple, and rose; 'Attar of Roses' is pictured. Fresh leaves are used in baking, cold drinks, and with fruit.

GROWING TIPS

Scented geraniums grow best in full sun and rich, light, well-drained soil. They prefer dry soil, but leaves will fall if it is too dry. Set plants into the garden in spring after frost danger has passed, and pinch out growing tips every few weeks to keep them bushy. Feed twice monthly with soluble fertilizer. In winter, bring plants indoors and keep them in full sun. Harvest leaves anytime and dry them on a screen in a cool dark place. Use dried leaves in teas and potpourris.

Perilla *(Perilla frutescens)*

Annual

The crisp, textured, green or reddish-purple foliage of Perilla, or Beefsteak Plant, has a metallic, bronzy sheen. Although it bears small spikes of lavender, pink, or white flowers in early fall, the plant is grown for its foliage, which earns it a place in the decorative garden. Plants grow 18–36 inches tall. Leaves are used fresh in salads and with fruit, and fresh flowers are used in fish dishes and soups. Perilla, especially the purple variety, is also used in stir-fry cooking.

GROWING TIPS

A tender annual, Perilla is set out after all danger of frost has passed in spring. Set plants 12–15 inches apart in full sun or light shade; transplant carefully if necessary, because the roots do not like to be disturbed. Soil should be dry, average to rich, and well drained. Pinch plants when they are 6 inches tall to encourage bushiness. Leaves can be picked anytime to use fresh or dried.

Parsley *(Petroselinum crispum)*

Biennial

Although biennial to zone 3, parsley is best grown as an annual because its foliage becomes bitter and tough in the second year. If parsley is grown as a biennial, flat clusters of yellowish-green flowers will bloom on 3-foot stems in the spring of the second year. Leaves are curled, crisped, or finely cut. Curly-leaf Parsley (pictured), with its rounded, crisped leaves, is prettier in the garden—and as a garnish—than Flat-Leaf Parsley. Parsley leaves are used fresh or dried to garnish almost any meat, egg, fish, or vegetable dish.

GROWING TIPS

Parsley can be grown from seeds, but these germinate slowly, so purchased plants often give better results. If you germinate your own seeds, soak them in water for 24 hours before sowing. Set parsley plants 6–8 inches apart, 2–4 weeks before the last spring frost, in full sun or light shade in rich, deep, moist, well-drained soil. Fertilize when plants are 4 inches tall and again a month later. Cut leaves with scissors; dry them on a screen, wrap in a paper towel and refrigerate, or roll in plastic wrap and freeze.

Scarlet Runner Bean *(Phaseolus coccineus)* Annual

Runner beans are close relatives of snap and lima beans, and are usually grown as annual decorative vines, although they do produce edible, foot-long beans. The red 1-inch flowers of this species, which is also called Flowering Bean and Painted Lady, are edible, too. They have a sweet bean taste and a crisp texture and are very good in salads, as garnishes, or floated on soups. Plants grow 8–12 feet tall and make an excellent screen on a wall or on a trellis.

GROWING TIPS

Sow the seeds of this tender annual outdoors where plants are to grow after all danger of frost has passed in spring. Plants should be thinned to 2 inches apart and given a warm spot in full sun and rich, moist, well-drained soil. Feed every month and keep well watered. Pick flowers as soon as they open and use them fresh.

Anise *(Pimpinella anisum)*

Anise seeds have been used through the centuries in breads, cookies, cakes, candies, and as a flavoring in Italian sausage. The leaves can be used, fresh or dried, in drinks, soups, and salads and are also said to aid digestion. A spreading, dainty, hardy plant, Anise has small, lacy leaves and grows 18–24 inches tall. Small, grayish-brown licorice-flavored seeds form after flat clusters of white flowers bloom in early summer.

GROWING TIPS

Anise prefers a spot in full sun where soil is light, sandy, neutral to slightly acid, and well drained. Water when the soil starts to become dry; do not over-water. Set out plants or sow seeds outdoors in early spring as soon as the soil can be worked, but transplant carefully as the roots do not like to be disturbed. Mound soil up around the base to support the stems. Pick leaves anytime. To harvest seeds, cut flowering stems 2–3 weeks after the flowers fade and hang the stems upside down in a paper bag.

Salad Burnet *(Poterium sanguisorba)* Perennial

Like Borage, Salad Burnet is often substituted for cucumbers in salads. This pretty perennial has finely cut leaves bunched at the base of the plant and sends up gracefully arching, 18- to 24-inch stems covered with small, toothed leaflets. Dense tufts of white or rose-pink flowers bloom in early summer to midsummer. The leaves have no flavor when dried, so if they are not used fresh, they are usually stored in vinegar—which then takes on a delightful cucumber flavor.

GROWING TIPS

Salad Burnet is hardy to zone 3. Where summers are very hot, plant in light shade; elsewhere, give it full sun. Soil must be poor, sandy, slightly alkaline, and well drained. Fertilize lightly if at all, or the leaves will lose their flavor; water only when the soil becomes dry. Plant or sow seeds anytime from mid-spring to midsummer, spaced 12–15 inches apart. Plants have a long taproot and may be difficult to transplant; they easily reseed and can become weedy. Harvest leaves whenever they are large enough.

Rose *(Rosa)*

The beauty of the rose garden or a cut rose is known to everyone, but fewer people realize that roses have a place in the kitchen garden or herb garden as well. Petals from fragrant roses are used to make pot-pourris, jelly, jam, pudding, and rose water. The rose hips, which are seedpods, are rich in vitamin C and are used in recipes for jelly, jam, tea, and toppings. Any fragrant rose petals can be used in recipes. All roses set hips, but the species ("wild") roses, shrub roses, and old garden roses set the greatest number. *Rosa rugosa rubra* is pictured.

GROWING TIPS

Roses should be planted in early spring, in full sun and rich, sandy, moist, well-drained soil. Hardiness varies from zones 3–8, depending on the type of rose and the variety. Winter protection is suggested for all. Trim or prune roses in spring. Cut flowers may be picked at any time for fresh use or for drying. To maximize the number of hips, do not remove flowers as they fade but allow them to set seeds.

Rosemary *(Rosmarinus officinalis)*

Perennial

Rosemary is hardy only to zone 8, so it is grown as an annual in many parts of the country. The 1- to 3-foot plants have long, flexible, aromatic stems covered with fragrant, gray-green, needlelike leaves. The leaves are used in all types of meat and poultry dishes, especially lamb. They are also used in potpourris, and a tea made with the leaves is said to be a good hair rinse. Whorls of pale blue flowers bloom on short spikes in winter where Rosemary is perennial; it may not bloom as an annual.

GROWING TIPS

Rosemary likes full sun or partial shade and light, slightly moist, well-drained soil. Plants can be set outdoors 2–4 weeks before the last spring frost, spaced 12–18 inches apart. Fertilize at planting time; where perennial, feed every spring when growth starts. Perennial plants can be divided, or the long stems can be layered. Winter protection is a good idea in all but the warmest climates. On hot summer days, mist the foliage. Cut plants back as necessary to keep them compact. Use leaves fresh or dried.

Garden Sorrel *(Rumex acetosa)*

Perennial

A perennial hardy to zone 4, Garden Sorrel is an erect, leafy plant forming large, dense clumps 12–18 inches high. The leaves are smooth, upright, and shaped like a lance or arrow. They have an acidic, lemony taste and are used in soups, salads, or baked fish. In late summer, 3-foot spikes of small off-white flowers appear.

Growing Tips

Plant seeds or plants in early spring or in fall, spacing them 12 inches apart. Soil should be rich and well drained. Cut plants to the ground once or twice during the growing season and feed and water to encourage new growth. Watering also encourages tender leaves, which are best used when young, as older leaves become quite tart and tough. To extend the harvest of the leaves, snap off flower stems as they begin to form. Pick leaves anytime and use them fresh.

Rue *(Ruta graveolens)*

Rue, known as the Herb of Grace, was used in ancient times to ward off witches with its powerful scent. A perennial hardy to zone 4, Rue is an attractive, shrubby evergreen with deeply cut, lacy, fernlike leaves. Clusters of buttonlike yellow flowers bloom in early summer to midsummer on 1½- to 3-foot-tall stems. Although Rue was once used medicinally, it is now thought that large quantities may be toxic. We recommend that it not be ingested. Instead, use it as a decorative plant or use its leaves in dried wreaths and decorations. Rue can cause an allergic reaction when handled, so wear gloves.

Growing Tips

Plant Rue in full sun and poor, moist, well-drained soil. Plants can go into the garden in spring as soon as the soil can be worked, spaced 6–12 inches apart. In spring, fertilize lightly, cut plants back to keep them compact, and divide if necessary. Just before frost, cut branches back and dry them on a screen.

Pineapple-scented Sage *(Salvia elegans)* Perennial

A perennial hardy only to zone 9, Pineapple-scented Sage is often grown as an annual. Plants grow 4–5 feet high where they are perennial and 3 feet high when grown as annuals. The leaves are dark green and rough; the tubular flowers are bright scarlet and bloom in late summer and fall. The foliage and flowers smell like pineapple and can be used fresh in teas, fruit dishes, salads, sandwiches, and desserts, or dried for teas, wreaths, and potpourris.

GROWING TIPS

Set plants into the garden in spring after all danger of frost has passed, spacing them 18–24 inches apart. Select a spot in full sun where the soil is light, sandy, and well drained. Where perennial, divide or cut back and fertilize in spring. When grown as an annual, fertilize at planting time; no other feeding is necessary. Where Pineapple-scented Sage is not hardy, plants can be dug in early fall and brought indoors. Cut entire branches to dry; fresh leaves can be picked at any time and dried on a screen if desired.

Sage *(Salvia officinalis)*

Since the days of the Roman legions sage has been used in teas, but it is more widely used today in poultry stuffing and sausages. It is a shrubby perennial with oblong, woolly leaves and hairy stems. Spikes of blue-violet, pink, or white flowers bloom in late spring and early summer on 2- to 2½-foot plants. Quite hardy, sage will grow as far north as zone 3 as long as it is not over-harvested. 'Tricolor', pictured, is a pretty variety with leaves of green, pink, and purple.

GROWING TIPS

Sage prefers a spot in full sun or light shade where soil is light, sandy, and well drained. Soil should be kept evenly moist during the summer, but must be dry during the winter. Plant in early spring, spacing plants 12–18 inches apart. Sage can be divided in spring or layered in early fall. In early spring, cut plants back to keep them bushy and fertilize lightly. Pick leaves before the plant blooms and again in late summer, and dry them on a screen. Harvest no more than the top third of the plant.

American Elderberry *(Sambucus canadensis)* Shrub

We may think of American Elderberry shrubs only as a source of berries for wines and jellies, but the flowers are also edible. Fresh flowers are used in fritters, and the dried flowers in teas. Elderberry (or elder) plants grow very quickly to 6–10 feet tall and have brittle branches covered with compound leaves. Hardy to zone 4, the plants form 6-inch, flat-topped clusters of white flowers in early summer, followed in late summer by the purplish-black berries.

GROWING TIPS

American Elderberry plants like full sun to partial shade and will grow in any soil, although they prefer moist conditions. They tend to sprawl and can be cut back to the ground at any time if they become too large for the garden. Pick the flowers as soon as they open for fresh use or for drying. Remember, if you cut all the flowers, you won't have any berries. Some varieties are inedible, and some wild relatives are toxic to humans. Never use the flowers or berries of an elderberry unless you are sure it is edible.

Winter Savory *(Satureja montana)*

A stiff, spreading plant, Winter Savory has thick, narrow, gray-green leaves with a strong, peppery flavor that are used fresh or dried to flavor beans and other vegetables. Hardy to zone 5, Winter Savory has loose spikes of pink or white flowers on 6- to 12-inch plants in summer. A close relative, Summer Savory *(Satureja hortensis),* is an annual with the same growing needs; its leaves have a more delicate flavor and are used in cooking to cut the odor of cabbage and turnips.

GROWING TIPS

Plant Winter Savory in full sun in light, sandy, slightly rich, well-drained soil. Water as soon as the soil starts to dry out to keep it evenly moist. Plants can go into the garden 4 weeks before the last spring frost. Each spring, fertilize when growth starts and divide plants if necessary. Pinch branch tips to encourage bushiness; prune in fall or spring. Propagate by layering in summer and transplant the next spring. Pick leaves before the flowers open and dry them on a screen in a cool place.

Alexanders *(Smyrnium olusatrum)* Biennial

Also known as Black Lovage or Horse Parsley, Alexanders is not as widely grown today as it was years ago. The large, celerylike biennial is hardy to zone 3 and grows 3–5 feet tall. The dark stems are topped by large, shiny, 3-part leaves and clusters of white to yellow flowers that bloom in the summer of the second year. The leaves, stems, and flower buds are edible and can be used fresh in salads; stems and leaves can be cooked like celery.

GROWING TIPS

Plant Alexanders in full sun in rich, sandy, well-drained soil. Seeds should be started outdoors in late summer and seedlings transplanted to their permanent position in fall. Mulch over the winter. The following year, feed and water frequently. When plants are 12 inches tall, snap off outer stems and leaves for cooking. In midsummer, prune the plants to keep them from growing to more than 24 inches. In fall, before harvesting, cover plants with tall baskets for 1–2 weeks to blanch the leaves and stem tips.

Common Lilac *(Syringa vulgaris)*

Shrub

Lilac flowers are well known for their delicious scent, which carries over into their taste. Lilacs have been used traditionally in fritters and can also be candied, used in herb butters, or used as garnishes for soups, salads, desserts, and hors d'oeuvres. Flowering in late spring, the shrubs grow to 15 feet in height and have heart-shaped leaves and pyramidal clusters of lavender, purple, or white flowers. Lilacs are hardy to zone 4.

Growing Tips

Grow lilacs in full sun and average, well-drained soil. They are subject to mildew and should be planted where air circulation is good. In early spring, prune away any weak wood, any wood that does not bear large flower buds, and suckers that have developed. Fertilize every other year. Any flowers not picked should be cut off as soon as they have faded. For culinary use, pick flowers as soon as they are open.

Winter Tarragon *(Tagetes lucida)* Perennial

Winter Tarragon is used as a substitute for French Tarragon in zone 10, where winters are not cold enough for French Tarragon. Winter Tarragon can be grown as an annual or a houseplant in other areas. Related to the garden marigold, Winter Tarragon grows 1–2 feet high and has narrow leaves of medium green that have a slightly sweet anise flavor. In fall or winter, plants bear small yellow flowers with a central tuft surrounded by a single row of petals.

GROWING TIPS

Plant Winter Tarragon outdoors after all danger of frost has passed. Select a spot with full sun and sandy, rich, well-drained soil that is kept evenly moist. In areas colder than zone 10, move plants indoors in fall or take cuttings to grow them as houseplants. Winter Tarragon is best used fresh; snip off the upper 3–6 inches of branch tips for the most tender leaves.

Dwarf Marigold *(Tagetes tenuifolia)*   Annual

Sometimes called Signet Marigold, this species is related to the better-known African and French marigolds. Dwarf Marigolds grow 8–10 inches high and bear lemon-scented foliage that is finer and lacier than that of other marigolds. The single flowers, which are 1 inch across, are gold, yellow, or orange. Although all marigold flowers are edible, they do not all taste good; 'Tangerine Gem', pictured, and 'Lemon Gem' have the most pleasant flavor. They can be used fresh as garnishes and dried to make a vitamin-rich tea.

GROWING TIPS

Marigolds like a spot in full sun where the soil is moderately fertile, moist, and well drained. They are easy to grow from seeds started indoors or in the garden; they should be spaced about 6 inches apart. Since they are tender, they should not be planted until all danger of frost has passed. Pick flowers as soon as they open and use them fresh or dried. The petals should be removed from the rest of the flower, which has a bitter taste, and dried on a screen.

Tansy (*Tanacetum vulgare* var. *crispum*) Perennial

Hardy to zone 3, tansy is a dramatic, 2- to 3-foot plant with attractive, fernlike, dark green 3- to 5-inch foliage. Buttonlike yellow flowers bloom in clusters in late summer. The leaves have a bitter flavor and at one time were used in both Passover seders and Lenten recipes. Today, the ingestion of tansy is no longer recommended, because it is believed to be toxic. Both leaves and flowers can be dried for arrangements, potpourris, and sachets; they are also used to repel insects. When planted near the house, tansy will keep ants from coming indoors.

GROWING TIPS

Tansy prefers full sun and rich, moist, well-drained soil. Set plants 12–18 inches apart, adding them to the garden border in mid-spring. Divide plants in either spring or fall when necessary and fertilize in spring when growth starts. Tansy spreads rapidly by underground runners; to keep it in bounds, thin it yearly or grow it in a container. Cut stems before the flowers are fully open and hang them upside down in a dark, dry place.

Lemon Thyme *(Thymus × citriodorus)*

Perennial

A cousin of culinary thyme, Lemon Thyme is a creeping plant that grows 8 inches high and spreads to 24 inches across. Numerous short, soft, erect stems rise from runners that grow along the ground and root at the nodes. Hardy to zone 8, the plant has spikes of pale lilac flowers in summer. The leaves are small, shiny, oval, and dark green, and have a delicious lemony fragrance. They can be used fresh or dried in broths or soups, added just before serving. Golden Thyme, shown here, makes a delicious herbal tea.

Growing Tips

Plant Lemon Thyme in full sun where soil is light, sandy, dry, and well-drained; it tolerates gravelly soil. Set plants into the garden, 10 inches apart, in spring or summer. In spring, divide if necessary, prune back to encourage compactness, and fertilize with cottonseed meal or bone meal. Propagate new plants by layering in summer and transplant in spring. Apply winter protection in cold areas, or grow plants as annuals. Cut branch tips anytime and use the leaves fresh, or dry them on a screen in a warm place.

Thyme *(Thymus vulgaris)*

Cultivated since ancient times, the genus *Thymus* includes more than 100 species and varieties, some of which are indispensable in the kitchen. Culinary thyme is used in poultry stuffing and soups, and in egg, meat, and vegetable dishes. Thyme is a woody spreading perennial, hardy to zone 5, that grows 6–12 inches tall. The leaves are small, aromatic, and gray-green; clusters of lilac-colored flowers bloom in spring and summer. Bees make a distinctive honey from thyme. *Thymus vulgaris*, pictured, is the most common in the kitchen garden.

GROWING TIPS

Thyme prefers full sun and light, sandy, dry, well-drained soil. Set plants into the garden in spring through summer, spaced 10 inches apart. Each spring, prune back to encourage compactness, fertilize with cottonseed meal or bone meal, and divide if necessary. Plants may be propagated by layering in summer and transplanted in fall or spring. Pick leaves anytime for fresh use, or take them just before the plants bloom and dry on a screen in a warm place.

Nasturtium *(Tropaeolum majus)* Annual

The young leaves, flower buds, and flowers of Nasturtium have a delicious, nippy, somewhat peppery taste and are a zesty and colorful addition to green salads. Nasturtium plants have dull, lobed, rounded gray-green leaves and funnel-shaped flowers of yellow, orange, or red that bloom all summer. Some varieties are bushy, growing about 12–18 inches high; others are trailing and can be grown in hanging baskets.

GROWING TIPS

Sow Nasturtium seeds outdoors after all danger of frost has passed, as the tender seedlings do not transplant well. Plant 8–12 inches apart in full sun to light shade and light, sandy, dry soil that is poor but well drained. Planting Nasturtiums in rich soil results in lush foliage but no flowers. Nasturtium grows best where nights are cool in summer. Snip off stems at ground level and use the foliage, buds, or flowers fresh. Cut off the bitter-tasting base of the flowers before using.

Tulip *(Tulipa)*

Bulb

Not only are they beautiful, tulip flowers are edible, too, and taste something like peas. They can be stuffed with chicken or tuna salad, cottage cheese, and other fillings. The best tulips to use in the kitchen are large, single-flowered hybrids in the groups called Darwin, Darwin Hybrid, Fosteriana, Triumph, or Cottage; pictured is 'Purissima', a Fosteriana tulip. All grow on 1½- to 3-foot stems and bloom in mid-spring or late spring.

Growing Tips

Plant tulip bulbs in late fall in full sun or partial shade. They should be planted at least 6 inches deep and 6 inches apart, in sandy, rich, well-drained soil. Fertilize when shoots start to emerge in spring. Tulips are hardy to zone 4, but must have cold winters to grow well, so refrigerate bulbs for 2–3 weeks before planting in zones 8–10. Do not remove the foliage after flowering until it has completely browned. Pick flowers when they first open, discard the stamens and pistils from the inside, and use fresh.

Sweet Violet *(Viola odorata)*

Perennial

Sweet Violets, which are sometimes called English Violets, are highly fragrant and have a strong, sweet flavor. The flowers can be candied or used fresh to decorate cakes. They can also be used fresh in fruit salads or floated on iced drinks. Perennial to zone 6, Sweet Violets have white, blue, or deep violet, 1-inch flowers on 4- to 8-inch tufted plants. The cultivar 'White Czar' is shown here. When grown as perennials, Sweet Violets bloom in spring; they can also be grown as annuals and will bloom in spring to early summer.

GROWING TIPS
Grow Sweet Violets in partial shade unless temperatures are very high, in which case they prefer full shade. Set plants 6–8 inches apart in early spring in rich, moist, well-drained soil and mulch to keep the soil cool. Feed every month when the plants are in growth or in flower. Cut the flowers when they first open and remove the stem behind the flower before serving.

Pansy (Viola × Wittrockiana) Annual

Pansies have a grassy flavor and are milder than Sweet Violets, but are edible and can be used in much the same way as violets: as garnishes, on desserts, and floating on iced drinks or soups. The flowers, which come in every color, are dainty, flat, 2–4 inches across, and often have "faces." Plants grow about 6–9 inches tall. The cultivar 'Clear Crystal Mix' is shown.

GROWING TIPS
Pansies can be set into the garden in very early spring as soon as the soil can be worked. They are hardy where winter temperatures do not drop below 20° F, so can be planted in the fall and mulched over winter for an even earlier spring bloom. They prefer full sun, but will tolerate light shade, and must have rich, moist, well-drained soil. Mulch roots in early spring to keep them cool. Pansies are long-lived where nights are cool, even if days are hot. To extend the blooming period, plant heat-resistant types and keep the flowers picked. Pinch them back if they become leggy. Pick flowers when they first open and use fresh.

APPENDICES

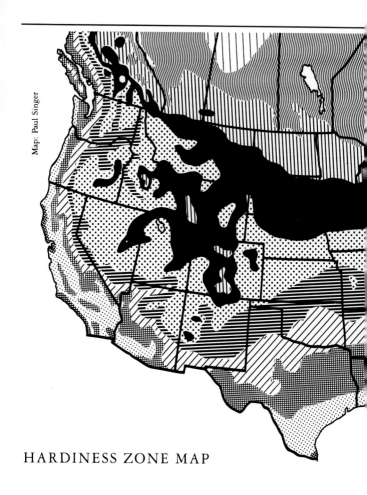

Map: Paul Singer

HARDINESS ZONE MAP

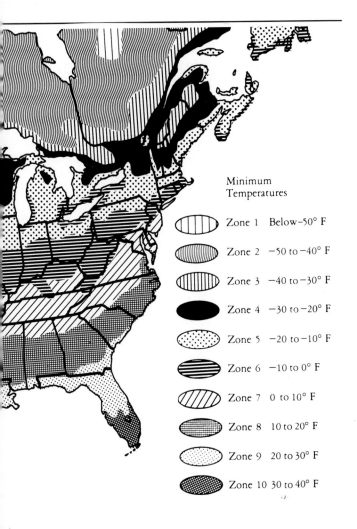

Minimum Temperatures

Zone 1 Below −50° F

Zone 2 −50 to −40° F

Zone 3 −40 to −30° F

Zone 4 −30 to −20° F

Zone 5 −20 to −10° F

Zone 6 −10 to 0° F

Zone 7 0 to 10° F

Zone 8 10 to 20° F

Zone 9 20 to 30° F

Zone 10 30 to 40° F

GARDEN PESTS AND DISEASES

Plant pests and diseases are a fact of life for a gardener. Therefore, it is helpful to become familiar with common pests and diseases in your area and to learn how to control them.

Symptoms of Plant Problems

Because the same general symptoms are associated with many diseases and pests, some experience is needed to determine their causes.

Diseases

Both fungi and bacteria are responsible for a variety of diseases ranging from leaf spots and wilts to root rot, but bacterial diseases usually make the affected plant tissues appear wetter than fungi do. Diseases caused by viruses and mycoplasma, often transmitted by aphids and leafhoppers, display such symptoms as mottled yellow or deformed leaves and twisted or stunted growth.

Insect Pests

Numerous insects attack plants. Sap-sucking insects—including aphids, leafhoppers, whiteflies, and scale insects—suck plant juices. The affected plant becomes yellow, stunted, and misshapen. Aphids and scale insects produce honeydew, a sticky substance that attracts ants and sooty mold fungus growth. Other pests with rasping-sucking mouthparts, such as thrips and spider mites, scrape plant tissue and then suck the juices that well up in the injured areas.

Leaf-chewers, namely beetles and caterpillars, consume plant leaves, whole or in part. Leaf miners make tunnels within the leaves, creating brown trails and causing leaf tissue to dry. In contrast, borers tunnel into shoots and stems, and their young larvae consume plant tissue, weakening the plant. Some insects, such as various grubs and maggots, feed on roots, weakening or killing the plant.

Nematodes

Microscopic roundworms called nematodes are other pests that attack roots and cause stunting and poor plant growth. Some kinds of nematodes produce galls on roots, while others produce them on leaves.

Snails and Slugs

Unfortunately, snails and slugs like fresh herbs as much as we do. They usually hide underground or in mulch or debris during the day and feed at night. There are several ways to get rid of them: Go out at night and pick them off by hand; sink saucers of beer up to their rims in the dirt; save the skins of grapefruit halves and invert them in the garden, checking for the pests every morning; or use bait or traps, available at garden centers.

Environmental Stresses

Some types of plant illness result from environment-related stress, such as severe wind, drought, flooding, or extreme cold. Other problems are caused by salt toxicity, rodents, birds, nutritional deficiencies or excesses, fertilizer burn, pesticides, or damage from lawn mowers. Many of these injuries are avoidable if you take proper precautions.

Controlling Plant Problems

Always buy healthy disease- and insect-free plants, and select resistant varieties when available. Check leaves and stems for dead areas or off-color and stunted tissue. Before you plant your herbs and edible flowers, be sure to prepare the soil properly.

Routine Preventives

By cultivating the soil routinely you will expose insects and disease-causing organisms to the sun and thus lessen their chances of surviving in your garden. In the fall, be sure to destroy infested or diseased plants, remove dead leaves and flowers, and clean up plant debris. Do not add diseased or infested material to the compost pile. Spray plants with water from time to time to dislodge insect pests and remove suffocating dust. Pick off the larger insects by hand. To discourage fungal leaf spots and blights, always water plants in the morning and allow the leaves to dry off before nightfall. For the same reason, provide adequate air circulation around leaves and stems by spacing plants properly.

Weeds provide a home for insects and diseases, so pull them up or use pre-emergent herbicides (we do not recommend the use of any other type). If you use weed-killers on your lawn, do not apply them too close to your herb garden or spray them on a windy day.

Insecticides and Fungicides

To protect plant tissue from injury due to insects and diseases, a number of insecticides and fungicides are available. However, few products control diseases due to bacteria, viruses, and mycoplasma. Pesticides are usually either "protectant" or "systemic" in nature. Protectants keep insects or disease organisms away from uninfected foliage, while systemics move through the plant and provide some therapeutic or eradicant action as well as protection. Botanical insecticides such as pyrethrum and rotenone have a shorter residual effect on pests, but are considered less toxic and generally safer for the user and the environment than inorganic chemical insecticides. Biological control through the use of organisms like *Bacillus thuringiensis* (a bacterium toxic to moth and butterfly larvae) is effective and safe.

Recommended pesticides may vary to some extent from region to region. Consult your local Cooperative Extension Service or plant professional regarding the appropriate material to use. Always check the pesticide label to be sure that it is registered for use on the pest with which you are dealing and is safe for use on edible plants. Follow the label concerning safety precautions, dosage, frequency of application, and the preharvest interval—the period to wait between spraying a pesticide on an edible plant and harvesting it.

HARVESTING HERBS AND
EDIBLE FLOWERS

ALMOST AS SOON as your herbs and edible flowers are in the ground, you can begin harvesting—there is no need to wait for a special harvest season for the fresh leaves and flowers of many plants. Others, of course, are best harvested at a particular time (as indicated in the plant descriptions), but for the most part, you will be able to reap the fresh bounty of your garden all season long.

Using Fresh Herbs

You can pick the leaves of most herbs at any time for fresh use. Harvest healthy leaves as you need them; pick them on a sunny morning after the dew has dried, rinse them, and pat them dry. Do not remove more than half the leaves at one time, and be careful not to injure the stems. Plants that have grown tall and lanky can be sheared back in midsummer and their leaves used fresh or dried. Leaves that are to be used dried should be picked before the flowers open, when they have the most flavor.

When using fresh herbs for teas or recipes that call for dried herbs, use two to three times the amount listed. Herbs lose their flavor quickly when heated and should be added to cooked foods near the end of the preparation time.

Drying Herbs

One method of drying herbs is to cut the stems back and, after washing them and patting them dry, hang them upside down; then remove the leaves when they have dried. Another method is to remove the leaves from the stems first, wash and pat dry, and spread them on a raised rack or screen. For both methods, select a dark, dry spot with good air circulation.

Leaves can also be dried in a microwave, placed between two paper towels. The time varies with the herb and the oven; start with two minutes and adjust if necessary. Some leaves can also be dried between sheets of waxed paper in the pages of a heavy book.

Some herbs lose their flavor when air dried. Basil, Chervil, fennel, burnet, and chives should be frozen. Parsley and dill lose their color when air dried; place them in the refrigerator in a moist paper towel instead.

One way you can make your dried herbs last is to use them in potpourri—a mixture of dried flower petals (usually roses) and the dried leaves and flowers of any fragrant herb. You can purchase essential oils to enhance the aroma and fixatives make it last.

Harvesting Seeds

Harvest seeds when they mature, which is usually several weeks after the flowers fade. Cut the stems before the seeds fall and hang them upside down in a dry spot with good air circulation. Place a paper bag over the seed heads to collect the seeds as they fall. Seeds retain more flavor if stored whole; you can grind or crush them later, when the time comes to use them.

Harvesting and Drying Flowers

In most cases, flowers should be cut for drying when they are about a third open (although there are exceptions—notably edible flowers; see below). Cut them in the morning, after the dew has dried, and dry them in the same manner as described above for leaves. If you are drying them for decorative purposes (not for ingestion), some will dry well in a desiccant such as silica gel.

Edible flowers should be cut as soon as they are fully open (unless you are using the buds). Put them in water if you are not going to use them immediately. Remove the stamens, pistils, and the white section at the base of the petals (if there is one) before ingesting them.

Using Edible Flowers

Edible flowers can add color, texture, and flavor to many dishes. As a general rule, use sweet or floral-scented blooms on desserts or to garnish cold drinks; use other flowers according to their flavor—in salads, floated in soups, and to garnish entrées. Nasturtiums, which are peppery, add tang to salads; mild-flavored tulips can be stuffed with cold fillings such as chicken salad. A favorite Italian dish is zucchini blossoms stuffed with herbs and ricotta cheese. You can mix flower petals with sweet butter, which will take on the flavor of the blooms you use: try pansies, roses, or calendulas. It is simple to preserve sweet violets, lilacs, pansies, and other sweet-smelling blooms by dipping them in egg white and sugar; use them to garnish cakes or ice cream.

Storing Herbs and Flowers

After drying them, store leaves, flowers, and seeds in the dark in an airtight container. Keep them away from heat—don't store them on a rack over the oven or on top of the refrigerator. Many herbs and flowers can be preserved in oil or vinegar. Some good herb vinegars include tarragon, basil, and burnet.

GLOSSARY

Acid soil
Soil with a pH value lower than 7.

Alkaline soil
Soil with a pH value of more than 7.

Annual
A plant whose entire life span, from sprouting to flowering and producing seeds, is encompassed in a single growing season.

Axil
The angle between a leafstalk and the stem from which it grows.

Basal leaf
A leaf at the base of a stem.

Biennial
A plant whose life span extends to two growing seasons, sprouting in the first growing season and then flowering, producing seed, and dying in the second.

Bolting
The premature or unwanted production of flowers and seeds, often caused by excessive heat.

Bract
A modified and often scalelike leaf, usually located at the base of a flower, a fruit, or a cluster of flowers or fruits.

Bud
A young and undeveloped leaf, flower, or shoot.

Bulb
A short underground stem, the swollen portion consisting mostly of fleshy, food-storing scale leaves.

Compost
A blend of decomposed organic matter not yet reduced to humus; soil or sand are sometimes added.

Compound leaf
A leaf made up of two or more leaflets.

Creeping
Prostrate or trailing over the ground or over other plants.

Cross-pollination
The transfer of pollen from one plant to another.

Crown
That part of a plant between the roots and the stem, usually at soil level.

Cultivar
An unvarying plant variety, maintained by vegetative propagation or by inbred seed.

Cutting
A piece of plant without roots; set in a rooting medium, it develops roots and is then potted as a new plant.

Deciduous
Dropping its leaves; not evergreen.

Disbudding
The pinching off of selected buds to benefit those left to grow.

Division
Propagation by division of crowns, roots, or tubers into segments that can be induced to send out roots.

Double-flowered
Having more than the usual number of petals, usually arranged in extra rows.

Drooping
Pendant or hanging, as in the branches of a weeping willow.

Evergreen
Retaining leaves for most or all of an annual cycle.

Genus
A group of closely related species; plural, genera.

Germinate
To sprout.

Herb
A plant without a permanent, woody stem, usually dying back during cold weather.

Herbaceous perennial
An herb that dies back each fall, but sends out new shoots and flowers for several successive years.

Horticulture
The cultivation of plants for ornament or food.

Humus
Partly or wholly decomposed vegetable matter; an important constituent of garden soil.

Hybrid
A plant resulting from a cross between two parent plants belonging to different species, subspecies, or genera.

Invasive
Aggressively spreading from the site of cultivation.

Layering
A method of propagation in which a stem is pegged to the ground and covered with soil and thus induced to send out roots.

Leaflet
One of the subdivisions of a compound leaf.

Loam
A humus-rich soil containing up to 25 percent clay, up to 50 percent silt, and less than 50 percent sand.

Lobe
A segment of a cleft leaf or petal.

Margin
The edge of a leaf.

Mulch
A protective covering spread over the soil around the base of plants to retard evaporation, control temperature, or enrich the soil.

Neutral soil
Soil that is neither acid nor alkaline, having a pH value of 7.

Node
The place on the stem where leaves or branches are attached.

Peat moss
Partly decomposed moss, rich in nutrients and with a high water retention, used as a component of garden soil.

Perennial
A plant whose life span extends over several growing seasons and that produces seeds in several growing seasons.

pH
A symbol for the hydrogen ion content of the soil, and thus a means of expressing the acidity or alkalinity of the soil.

Pollen
Minute grains containing the male germ cells and released by the stamens.

Propagate
To produce new plants, either by vegetative means involving the rooting of pieces of a plant, or by sowing seeds.

Prostrate
Lying on the ground; creeping.

Rhizome
A horizontal underground stem, distinguished from a root by the presence of nodes and often enlarged by food storage.

Rootstock
The swollen, more or less elongate, underground stem of a perennial herb; a rhizome.

Rosette
A crowded cluster of leaves; usually basal, circular, and at ground level.

Runner
A prostrate shoot that roots at its nodes.

Seed
A fertilized, ripened ovule, almost always covered with a protective coating and contained in a fruit.

Self-sow
To reproduce by dropping seeds.

Semidouble
Having more than the usual number of petals.

Semievergreen
Retaining at least some green foliage well into winter, or shedding leaves only in cold climates.

Species
A population of plants or animals whose members are at least potentially able to breed with each other, but which is reproductively isolated from other populations.

Spike
An elongated flower cluster whose individual flowers lack stalks.

Taproot
The main, central root of a plant.

Terminal
Borne at the tip of a stem or shoot, rather than in the axil.

Till
To work the soil into small fragments.

Toothed
Having the margin divided into small, toothlike segments.

Tuber
A swollen, mostly underground stem that bears buds and serves as a storage site for food.

Tufted
Growing in dense clumps, cushions, or tufts.

Two-lipped
Having two lips, as in certain irregular flowers.

Variegated
Marked, striped, or blotched with some color other than green.

Variety
A population of plants that differs consistently from the typical form of the species, either occurring naturally or produced in cultivation.

Vegetative propagation
Propagation by means other than seed.

Whorl
A group of three or more leaves or shoots, all emerging from a stem at a single node.

PHOTO CREDITS

G. R. Roberts, 39, 53

John J. Smith, 43

Steven M. Still, 28, 29, 33, 34, 38, 40, 55, 58, 77, 92

David M. Stone, 65

George Taloumis, 76

Mary M. Thacher, PHOTO RESEARCHERS, INC., 41

George Whiteley, PHOTO RESEARCHERS, INC., 74

INDEX